Acc

BETTER

MW00611067

"Everyday I am amazed at the way my new perspective is fueling creative energy and giving me the courage to make the career moves I had been hesitant to make. My career is at a new high thanks to **Better Choices.** "

—*Anthony Page, Playwright*

"Dr. Hargrove has the unique ability to take a complex and challenging issue and make it simple and easy. This book is truly a gift for all. A must read that will change your life!"

—*Steven Kaplan, Owner, Sunshine Bakery*

"I love the Mabel and Sonja stories at the beginning of each chapter—especially the story about letting go of fear. I could really put myself in Sonja's shoes and learn from Grandma Mabel."

—*Jessica Pruitt, Student*

"It is absolutely true! When our students know better, they do better. I experienced the power of the Decision Reframing Program with the changes that occurred in the students at our alternative school. The balloon process is a breakthrough approach to working with students with difficult life challenges."

—*Winnette Bradley, Director of Alternative Education*
Richmond County School System

"When members of my family were tragically killed in a car accident, we literarily shut down. We couldn't even move forward to participate in planning the funeral arrangements. With the balloon process our family was able to get past the pain and become functional again. I am truly grateful to Faye Hargrove and her work. "   —*Rev. Bob Hale*

i

BETTER CHOICES

When We Know Better, We Do Better

FAYE HARGROVE, PHD

Foreword by Louise A. Rice, PhD

Peace & joy always

Faye Hargrove 2/14/10

Stewart and Associates, Inc.
118 Park Avenue SW, Suite 700
Aiken, South Carolina 29801

Wake up one morning you realize
Your life is one big compromise
Stuck in the job you swore was only temporary

Feel like the world is passin' you by
Never done the things you wanted to try
Stuck in one place, got a pain in your face
From all your stressing out

You ask yourself there's got to be more than what I'm livin'
for
You ask yourself there's got to be something else
Something more, more, more, well,

Let the sun shine on your face
And don't let your love life go to waste
Now is the time, you got to make up your mind
Let it shine on you, let it shine on you

Feel like there's nothing, nowhere to go
You try and fight but you can't let go
Of all the pain, got so much to gain
Now is the time

You ask yourself there's got to be somethin' else
Something more, more more...

CONTENTS

PART II CLEARING SPACE FOR BETTER CHOICES

FOREWORD

PEACE OF MIND IS NO SMALL GIFT

For more than three decades, I interacted with, taught, listened to, encouraged, and counseled many people— young and old, male and female, professional and non-professional—in both my role as a college professor and administrator and in leadership positions in Delta Sigma Theta Sorority, Inc. I have observed over the years that many of those who sought my advice could often see the end of the road and envision a better life for themselves, but they, like a car with all four wheels embedded in ten or more inches of muddy red clay, were stuck. They could envision themselves on drier and higher ground and crossing the finish line, but they did not know how to make the right moves to get there.

Faye Hargrove has been gifted with an insightful perspective that assists each of us to overcome negative thoughts and influences in our life and to claim the power of positivity with which we have been blessed. She is the perfect coach for the stuck, broken, bitter, and unfulfilled. For over twenty-five years, she has used her professional expertise to help her clients—which include students, artists, executive leaders, ministers, military men and women, serious and violent offenders, and others of all ages and from all walks of life. In a life-changing fashion, she has helped them to identify and overcome obstacles that were preventing them from being truly happy and from succeeding.

Now, she has put in writing the remarkable personal breakthrough program that has moved so many from the "but, but, but" excuses mode to the "I know I can, I know I can" mode! This book, **Better Choices**, is to be experienced, not just read. It offers a 'tried and true' program for making appropriate choices in your daily living, as the title suggests. I can attest to the effectiveness of this program which demonstrates that "when we know better, we do better." I personally experienced the balloon process to let go grief after the loss of my husband, initially, and to overcome my fear of lizards, later.

Better Choices is filled with gems of wisdom—from the stories of Grandma Mabel and her granddaughter Sonja, which introduce each chapter, to the techniques for SMART goal-setting. With the accompanying CDs, Dr. Hargrove's voice gently guides you through the "letting go" and reframing process in a very assuring and comforting manner.

Whether you are hampered by anger, hostility, resentment, sadness, fear, shame, grief, guilt, or limited beliefs, you will find good, plain, solid wisdom that will enable you to "let go" of the negative influences in your life that obstruct your success and to capture the positive forces that will allow you to take charge of your life. It is my sincere hope that this book will reach the hands and desks of everyone who needs a breakthrough and the believing attitude of "I know I can, I know I can."

Louise A. Rice, Ph.D.
CEO, It's Writefully Correct
&
23rd National President
Delta Sigma Theta Sorority, Inc.

ACKNOWLEDGEMENTS

I owe a debt of gratitude to the many people who have contributed to the completion of this book. First, I would like to thank those who trusted my early work with the Decision Reframing Process (DRP). These include Dr. Dana Beden; Winnette Bradley; and the Richmond County Board of Education; along with Ted Wiggins, formerly of the Georgia Department of Corrections Probations Office.

Thanks to Dr. Robin Fivush, Chair of the Psychology Department at Emory University, for reminding me to focus on the fact that the DRP works and to let others build promotion and tenure files by determining *why* it works. To Dr. Tad James, whose work in Neurolinguistic Programming (NLP) inspired both the DRP and the use of the Grandma Mabel metaphors in each chapter; to Dr. Louise Rice for her sisterly encouragement and professional manuscript corrections; to Debra Starks-Patrick, whose transformation made my purpose clear; to Mark Alison, Linda Motto, and the staff at the Alison Group; to Marlon Stokes, a brilliant young musician and composer; and to those who reviewed and provided early input on the manuscript, I am extremely appreciative.

Finally, I am deeply grateful for my husband, Clarence, and his unwavering support and loving patience throughout the writing process; for my daughter, Chenille, and her wise counsel; and for my son, Cameron, who kept asking me, "When are you going to finish the book?"

I love you all!

Faye

INTRODUCTION

A FIRE SHUT UP IN MY BONES

I had been pregnant with this book for many years. The gestation period seemed to go on and on and on... ad infinitum until a series of events occurred within a six week period. Finally! I started the birthing process.

The thing about labor pains is that you know something big is about to happen. And it's going to happen in a very painful way. I felt the full pain of birthing this book while watching an episode of Oprah.

Let me explain. One day it just *happened* that I was home at a time of day when the Oprah Show was airing. The television is usually turned off, but for some reason it was going full blast on that day. From the next room I heard Oprah announce the topic and guests for the day. Because I am the ultimate Oprah fan (I even mimicked her hairstyles for a few years), I plopped down on the sofa to watch for a few minutes.

The focus of the show was overweight teenagers. Counselors Yvonne and Rich Dutra St. John led the young people in a workshop to uncover the truth behind their struggles with weight. They took the teens through an exercise to show them that they are not alone, to put them in touch with their emotions, and to gain tools to help them get feelings out instead of trying to *numb them* out through food.

Yvonne and Rich were very successful in helping the students tap into a place they call the "inner balloon"—a place inside where people hide the feelings they can't express. To help this group of teenagers express their inner anger, Yvonne and Rich had them participate in an exercise where they completed the sentence, *"I'm angry that..."*

I watched painfully as one student after another experienced an emotional meltdown in front of Oprah, the counselors, their parents, and all of the television audience. By the time a young girl named Jillian had her turn, I had reached my limit. I was actually sobbing and beginning to feel a great deal of anger of my own.

"Why can't you see that it is not necessary to put these children through all this pain?" I started yelling at the television. "Yes, you help them get in touch with their feelings of anger. So what? They are aware that they are angry. Now what?" As I watched this depressing scene unfold, I wanted the counselors to show these kids a way to let go of the anger without all this drama. "What is the problem with you people?" I shouted.

The moment I screamed the question, I felt a sudden sense of calm. I knew the answer. The water finally broke in my birthing process. (It is too bad I couldn't have felt the same calm when I was in labor birthing two children. I required Demerol for that!)

It was then that a quiet voice in my head said to me, "They don't know how to help the children in that way because you are still carrying inside of you the book describing the process. The Decision Reframing Process can help them, but you have to do your part and show them how."

From that moment on, I felt the urgency to write this book and to show the world how the Decision Reframing Process™ (DRP™, aka Balloon Process™) can transform so many lives. To quote the Prophet Jeremiah in the Christian Bible, this book, **Better Choices,** became *"like a fire, a fire shut up in my bones. I am weary of holding it in; indeed, I cannot."*

THE SOLDIERS ARE COMMITTING SUICIDE

Earlier during the week of the Oprah episode, the headline in the Augusta Chronicle, the local newspaper, read: "*Soldier suicide figures climb.*" I felt an early labor pain as I read about how the Army had announced that suicide rates among soldiers rose last year to the highest level in decades. The article called for more mental health professionals to sign up for the military because troops are "under tremendous and unprecedented stress." According to the news article, the most common factors for suicides were relationship problems, legal or financial issues, and problems on the jobs.

I thought of Beverly, a retired Army Captain who had worked with our firm a few years ago. Beverly served in Afghanistan, Guatemala, and several other overseas assignments during her tour of duty. She once told me, "It's just not the same when you come back home. You really need to have a way to shake that stuff."

After Beverly went through the DRP™ that is offered in this book, she trained in the process and learned to help her friends who were also wounded warriors, by one definition or another. None of them have committed suicide! Currently, Beverly is in graduate school working on a mental health degree.

REIGN OVER ME-THE FIRST SIGNS OF LABOR

A few days before reading the article in the paper about soldier suicide, I watched a rerun of the 2007 movie, **Reign Over Me**, starring Don Cheadle and Adam Sandler. The two actors play former college roommates, Alan and Charlie, who meet up again by chance on a Manhattan street corner five years after Charlie lost his family on 9/11. Charlie had been a successful dentist but he is unable to overcome the trauma of losing his family. Charlie has checked out on life. Full of guilt, grief and anger, he becomes so destructive that at one point in the movie Alan counsels his friend, "*Man, you just gotta let that shit go.*"

"He would, if he could," I said aloud to the television. "It's time for the book to be born."

THEY HAVEN'T LOCKED ME UP AGAIN

The birthing process actually started a few weeks before I saw the movie, read the article, or saw the overweight teenager episode of Oprah.

"Dr. Faye," said the voice on the office answering machine. "I just called to say thank you for the Christmas card and to let you know that I made my one-year anniversary. They haven't locked me up again. I'm doing just fine."

In 2007 and 2008, my firm worked with men being released from prison through a federal grant for the reentry of serious and violent offenders.[1] The voice on the answering machine was that of Carl, one of the parolees. My work with Carl and the others involved taking them through the DRP™, helping them to set educational and job goals, and coaching them through the process of reentry.

The DRP™ allowed them to release the stored negative emotions. Anger, hostility, fear, and insecurity often drove the decisions they made to commit criminal acts. This letting-go program also allowed them to handle anxiety associated with returning to the free world and trying to pick up the pieces.

The odds were against them. The recidivism rate for this population is extremely high. So when Carl (not his real name) called to say he was doing just fine after one year, I felt a great sense of satisfaction that our work had helped him to make the right kinds of choices. I was even more convinced that the world needed to be introduced to our model for helping these men to get back on track with their lives. I needed get this book written!

LEARNING TO LET IT GO

We can not change the events of the past. What has happened has happened. It is what it is. The past has no

---

[1] *Funded by the Departments of Justice, Labor, Education, Housing and Urban Development, and Health and Human Services, the Serious and Violent Offender Reentry Initiative (SVORI) supported innovative reentry programs at the state and community level.*

power except that we can learn from it. We can make peace with the past and accept it.

The good news is that we are able to change *how* we feel about events from our past. When we let go of our attachments to the feelings associated with the memories from the past, they no longer have the power to influence the decisions we make in our daily lives.

This book is about helping you to know that:

1. Who you are today and the circumstances of your life are the result of all the accumulated decisions you have made right up to this very minute.

2. Every decision you make is filtered through the frame that makes up your model of the world. Your model of the world, "the story of you," defines who you are today and helps you to make choices about how to experience each situation in you life.

3. You can change or *reframe* your model of the world by letting go of stored negative emotions and limiting beliefs that are associated with your past experiences.

4. Chapters 4-8 and the CD companions are tools to take you through the **Decision Reframing Process™ (DRP™)** so that you may let go of these stored emotions and limiting beliefs in a way that is safe and private.

5. You can make better choices when you have confidence in who you are and in your ability to make all your efforts successful.

MEET GRANDMA MABEL

Each chapter begins with an amusing story that is a dialogue between Mabel and her granddaughter Sonja. The stories are metaphors that are used because they are short stories that help the reader get the main idea of the chapter before potentially getting bogged down in the details. Describing the writing of this book as giving birth is an example of using a metaphor to make a point.

In each story, think of Mabel as the voice of the coach and Sonja as the reader or student. As Sonja understands the main point from Mabel's lesson, you will also get it!

WHAT DO I NEED FROM YOU?

Not much, really. Simply give yourself permission to get out of your own way and keep reading!

"We can't worry about what ain't happened yet. And we can't change what already was. What we got on our hands is today, right now. Times a wasting child, let's get started!" **—Grandma Mabel**

PART I

WE ALL COME FROM SOMEWHERE

CHAPTER 1

PRISONERS OF OUR PERSPECTIVES

Mabel and her granddaughter Sonja were walking on the path in the woods when Sonja noticed that the sky was getting dark and it looked as though it would rain soon. "Grandma, we should head for home. The sky looks dark," she said

Mabel looked at the sky with curiosity and wondered why Sonja was concerned. All she noticed was a beautiful day with puffy white clouds. The afternoon was perfect. "No it's not, Sonja. There is no rain coming. The weather report called for perfectly clear skies today," Mabel said.

"Grandma, I'm looking at the sky and I'm telling you. It is getting dark like it's going to rain! We should head for home now," Sonja persisted.

"Sonja," her grandmother said, "take off your sun glasses."

Sonja removed the dark shades. She squinted briefly and allowed her eyes to adjust to the light. "Oh," she laughed sheepishly. "I forgot I had these things on. I guess you are right, Grandma. When you look at the sky through the glasses it seems very dark. When I take them off, I can see that we have time to enjoy walking together for a little while longer!"

GRANDMA MABEL'S WISDOM

Grandma Mabel and Sonja were looking at the same sky but they drew different conclusions. When Sonja viewed the day through her dark sunglasses, she was convinced that the rain was coming and that she and her grandmother should head for home to avoid the bad weather. But Mabel had a very different perspective of the day. She advised Sonja to remove the shades and recognize that the day was just lovely.

Everyone views life and the circumstances of each day through his or her own set of lenses. Your perspective about issues helps you decide whether the glass is half empty or half full or whether the unknown is inviting and full of possibilities rather than mysterious and frightening. Like Sonja taking off her sun glasses, you have the powerful ability to change your lens and your perspective.

CHOOSING TO BE HAPPY

Suppose I asked you to make a list of the people you know who are genuinely happy and perfectly content with their lives. Maybe they see their lives as having purpose and as meaningful. They enjoy their work and find it satisfying. Think of your friends, your neighbors, the people you work with, and your family members. Of the people you know, how many names could you put on your list?

If you are like most of us, your list is relatively short. Why is it that so many of us are unhappy when we live in a country of unlimited resources and opportunities? As a nation we consume billions of tranquilizers, antidepressants, amphetamines, and pain killers every year. We sit through millions of hours of counseling and therapy sessions. We drink alcohol and take other drugs to numb ourselves and escape from lives that don't make us happy.

Imagine what the world would be like if you and everyone you know woke up one day and shouted out loud, "I love my life! Today, I choose to be happy!" You are probably thinking, "Yea right." If we could do that, we wouldn't need all those antidepressants and therapy sessions."

Before you dismiss the idea, play along with me for a little while. When I was a young girl, the teachers at the Butler Baker School that I attended would tell us, *"If your mind can conceive it, and your heart can believe it, then you can choose to achieve it."* At the time it seemed like just another corny phrase. However, five decades later, I can appreciate the power of those words.

I am especially moved by the notion that we are in control of the choices that shape our circumstances. Suppose you chose only to act and think in ways that brought you joy. Suppose you chose to behave in ways that helped you to grow, benefited the planet, and made your life better. If all the choices in your life had

> *Your life is built on every decision that you have made until this very moment.*

been made with these goals in mind, then you are one of the very few people who have chosen to be happy and fulfilled.

A CLOUD DOES NOT PUT OUT THE SUN

You may find that life is presenting you with some significant challenges right now. Perhaps you are feeling overwhelmed, confused, bitter, anxious or hurt. Although these feelings may seem to consume you and define your whole world at times, they are not who you really are. They are like clouds that may temporarily obscure the view of the sun. The clouds pass and we are able to see that the sun was there all along.

Your life is built on every decision that you have made until this very moment—from the decision to get out of bed, to what you will have for breakfast, to the kind of day you expect to experience. You make the decision, and then you spend the rest of the day defending and justifying your choice.

My hope is that your experience with this book will lead you to make every choice count toward a happy and fulfilling life. How, you ask? You will do this by recognizing the clouds and letting go of some bad habits and limited thinking. You will reframe the way you currently make choices and learn ways to take responsibility for creating your own happiness at every moment.

Sonja handed a card to her grandmother and whispered shyly, "Happy Mothers Day, Grandma."

"Oh, you are such a sweet child. Come here and give me some sugar. Grandma loves her sweet Baby Sonja!" Mabel held her arms out inviting her granddaughter to come closer.

"I love you too, Grandma. You're easy to love," Sonja said as she hugged Mabel tightly.

Mabel gently pushed Sonja away to arms length. She looked directly at her and said, "Oh, I haven't always been so easy to love, little girl. I was just as mixed up as some of the other members of this crazy family we belong to."

"Yes, we do have some characters in our family," Sonja laughed. "Like Uncle Jack, for example. I don't like to ask him how he is doing. All I can expect to hear from him is a series of moaning, whining and complaining. His sinuses, his arthritis, his gout! He has a doctor for every body part, you know. What a wet blanket. He can take the "J" right out of joy!"

"You're right," Mabel responded laughing at Sonja's accurate description of Jack. "Don't forget about Aunt VeeJay, Mabel added. "That woman can get on my very last nerve! She's so proper and righteous—always correcting everyone and bragging about the latest thing she bought at Saks Fifth Avenue."

"Yes, Uncle Jack and Aunt VeeJay are annoying, Grandma, but Cousin James really scares me," Sonja said. "He blows up so easily. I have to watch every word I say to him."

"James is a hurt and angry man," Mabel explained. "Since he has returned from serving in Iraq, he just can't seem to get back on track. It is too bad that he and Cathy are in the midst of getting a divorce."

"Grandma, I can't imagine that you were ever like Cousin James, or Aunt VeeJay, or Uncle Jack. You're just kidding me, right?"

"No, Baby. I'm not kidding with you."   Mabel's tone turned serious. "I was full of bitterness and hurt. On top of that, I didn't feel good about myself. I had to let go of all that stuff that was inside of me. It would have kept me from being the very best Grandma that I can be for my precious little Sonja."

Mabel stood akimbo. With her hands on her hips and her elbows bowed outward, it reminded Sonja of angels' wings.

"You're my angel, Grandma," Sonja said giving Mabel another hug.

MABEL'S WISDOM

Can you identify with Mabel's description of the members of her family? Maybe you even recognized yourself in Uncle Jack, Aunt VeeJay or Cousin James. Mabel believed that she acted like those relatives because of the "stuff" she was carrying around. Mabel's "stuff" consisted of the feelings of resentment, insecurity, and grief she held on to from painful memories. She thought of these stored negative emotions as baggage that caused her to act at times like her relatives. If she had not let go of the baggage, it would have gotten in the way of her ability to become the centered, loveable grandmother that Sonja adored.

EMOTIONAL COMPANIONS

You may be wondering why the focus of this book is on feelings about past events. Let's face it. We can't change the past, right?

Your emotions serve you in ways that keep you healthy and powerful. They are necessary and useful. There are times, however, when you allow your feelings to work against you in ways that are unhealthy. This happens most often when we store emotions from memories long after the event is over and done.

If you are still carrying around negative emotions attached to certain memories, they have a way of infiltrating your daily life---sometimes in unexpected ways. Past events in your life may trigger anger, frustration, fear, insecurity, hurt, mistrust, resentment, depression, rejection, shame, guilt, or other negative emotions today. Inappropriate emotional reactions, such as bursts of anger, periods of apathy, depression, sadness, anxiety, and chronic fear, often prevent people from achieving the quality of life they desire. Limiting decisions, such as "I'm not good enough," "I'll never get that promotion," or "I don't deserve a great marriage" create false limitations and hamper your ability to create reachable and attainable goals and outcomes. People smoke, drink, overeat, abuse other people, or take drugs often because they want to get away from uncomfortable feelings. Emotions we haven't let go of can also be the source of physical problems, like coronary heart disease, ulcers, and heart attack.

Although we cannot change what has already happened, we can actually change how we *feel* about what has happened. We can let go of the feelings, reframe the story we created at the time of those events, and also revise the decisions we made about how we should act in the future.

Because no one has ever taught you that it is possible to let go of painful, frightening, or angry feelings, you may be carrying those feelings around as your constant companions. These companions have an impact on your personality because every decision you make gets filtered through those emotions. They show up in your behavior in ways that might surprise you. Without even realizing it, you can wave a flag declaring that you are an insecure, sad, or angry person.

Over the years, I have had the privilege of assisting a great number of people and serving as their executive or personal development coach. I have noticed that if you pay close attention to what people say and do, the people with unresolved negative emotions can be easily identified.

Read the following descriptions of ten types of people that you may encounter every day. [2] Do you know any of these people? Have you ever behaved like one of these people?

1. **The Rut Dweller**—To the naked eye, the first group appears to be very ordinary, even successful people. They have families. They go to work everyday and wear all the trappings of the great American Dream. They may be educated, drive nice cars, and live in affluent neighborhoods. On the surface, these rut dwellers seem to have it all together. So what is missing in this picture?

   Rut dwellers are stuck. They have invested time and energy to get where they are only to realize they are empty and unfulfilled. Ruts can be jobs or relationships. Rut-dwellers want to make significant changes—get another job, start a business, go to school, leave a relationship, but they are afraid to make a move. They may know exactly what they want but they can't seem to get started making their dreams a reality. Or maybe they don't know where they want to go. They just know they don't want to be where they are—stuck.

2. **The Touchy-Defensive**—One of the most difficult groups to be around, supersensitive touchy-defensive people take every comment as a personal attack. They are argumentative verbal-brawlers. Because they think they already know everything, it is difficult to give feedback to these persons. Their insecurity causes them to come across as arrogant and uncooperative and they render themselves unteachable.

---

[2] These descriptions are not presented as personality disorders as described in the *Diagnostic and Statistical Manual of Mental Disorders.*

3. **The Bully**—Mean-spirited and angry, this group may be controlling, abusive, and manipulative partners who can ruin the self-esteem of others. As co-workers, they are unethical, and willing to damage co-workers to achieve their employment goals. On the street they are the criminals, con artists, and people-users who purposefully damage others. They may verbally bully and intimidate others with their temper tantrums.

4. **The Brokenhearted**—Faced with the death of a loved one or a great personal loss, the broken hearted feels like life is sitting on them like a 500-pound weight. They look for ways to make themselves feel better and avoid the discomfort of sadness and pain. They may turn to drugs and other means of medicating the pain away. Sometimes they give up on life altogether.

5. **The Diva**— Divas may be bossy, condescending, self-absorbed, and materialistic. They maintain themselves as the center of attention, build their own pedestals, and firmly plant themselves on top. Divas put a great emphasis on dressing up on the outside to deceive the world and hide a fragile sense of self on the inside. Gender does not matter. Men as well as women can display the diva personality where style wins out over substance.

6. **The Door Mat**—The world walks all over door mats. Door mats worry that if they aren't "nice" someone won't like them or they will upset someone. To keep this from happening, they martyr themselves and become what others need them to be. Because they feel unworthy, they put aside their own desires and feelings to give in to what others want. They may give up their identity, live in the shadow of others, or follow other people's agendas without question. In the interest of pleasing, door mats say yes when they really want to say no.

7. **The Victim**—"*They*" (outside forces) are the cause of all the trouble in the victims' lives. When things go wrong, it is never their fault. When something bad happens to them, they think it is part of a conspiracy; Victims blame and point fingers rather than take responsibility for their actions or for their lives. Expecting the government, their family, or some other outside force to take care of them, victims see themselves as powerless to affect their circumstances. "It's not my fault!" is their motto. Blame, bad luck, and excuses replace their efforts to take responsibility and *drive their own bus.* They view their victim status as making them entitled to receive special benefits or sympathies from others.

8. **The Wet Blanket**— They are whiny, pessimistic, and no fun to be around. The wet blanket has a "yea, but" response to every good idea. They expect the worst outcome and point out the down side to every situation. Their negativity shows up in their attitude toward their own health and they are often hypochondriacs. Because they assume the worst will happen, they do not take risks or venture far outside of their comfort zones.

9. **The Aloof**— Without a closer look, aloof persons would appear to be simply quiet and reserved loners. Or you may consider them to be shy. Actually, this group has deliberately built a firewall of social protection around themselves. Holding everyone at an emotional arms length, they do not venture beyond the walls or allow anyone to penetrate their barrier. You will not get close to the inner feelings of the cool aloof. Aloofs resist relationships that require them to emotionally commit or engage themselves at any significant level. They prefer to maintain detached shallow relationships.

10. **The Pre-Phoenix**— A phoenix is a mythical bird with a colorful plumage and a tail of gold and scarlet. It is said to have a 500 to 1,000 year life-cycle, near the end of which it builds itself a nest of myrrh twigs that then bursts into

flames. The nest and the bird burn to ashes. From the ashes a new, young phoenix arises, reborn anew to live again. The bird is also said to regenerate when hurt or wounded by a foe, thus being immortal and invincible. For the Phoenix, each rebirth offers the chance to torch old shabby feathers and rise again brilliant, rejuvenated and ready to soar.

The pre-phoenixes have yet to rise from the ashes. They are the men and women who find themselves at the *opposite* end of the American Dream spectrum. They include women who are transitioning off welfare and learning to face a life of self sufficiency, men exiting the prison system, displaced homemakers, or teenage parents with little education and little hope of leading lives like the people they see on TV or in movies. The pre-phoenixes have the ability to rise from the ashes but they may not feel confident enough to try.

The people who display these styles adopt them in response to frustrating, difficult, and painful situations and life experiences. Their decide how to react to life using these unresolved emotions as their filter. Are any of these people related to you? Is your boss or your co-worker in this group? At times, you may even see yourself in several of the characters described above. Maybe it's the wet blanket, or the broken-hearted, or even the rut-dweller.

In this book, you will learn to recognize when stored negative emotions cause you to act like one of the characters above. Once you recognize these constant companions and decision filters, you can break free and let them go. You will learn to use life's lessons to build and grow you rather than diminish or shut you down.

This is what I have learned:

1. *No one can block your success better than you can.* You don't have to worry about other people standing in your way or limiting you. You probably do a pretty good job of shutting yourself down.

2. *Changing old ineffective ways of thinking and behaving requires an inward journey.* You have to recognize and remove barriers like fear, bitterness, hostility, self-doubt, feelings of inadequacy, grief, depression, anxiety, and resentment. These stored emotions derail some lives and prevent others from getting a start at all.

3. *Setting goals is a lot easier when you can be optimistic about the future.* In Chapter 9, you will have the opportunity to set some SMART goals for your future. We won't even attempt to do this until after you have changed your perspective on what kind of future is possible. Clearing out the past will set the stage for putting goals in your future.

Case Study: What do you want?

"What do you want?" is not always an easy question to answer when the response is filtered through past disappointments. In our Next Steps Program,[3] my staff and I worked with a group of teenagers who were assigned to the alternative school as a disciplinary measure. For the most part, they had been labeled "problem kids." I found that if I asked this group of students what they wanted to do with their lives, very few were willing to tell me, especially in front of their peers. Was it because they had no clue about their future? Actually, that was not the case.

After they were able to reframe the belief systems that had them too fearful to put their hopes in a dream, they told

---

[3] Hargrove Leadership Services piloted Project Next Steps™ in the Richmond County School System in spring 2008. The program targeted chronic rule violators and students at risk of dropping out. Students who went through the HLS Decision Reframing Program experienced fewer disciplinary incidences and improved their attendance record.

me of wonderful plans they had constructed for their lives—plans to become veterinarians, own an auto repair shop, become a pediatrician, or own a hair salon. Not one person ever told me that she wanted to live a humdrum life full of frustrations and *I-wish-I-couldas!* Setting goals is a lot easier when you can be optimistic about the future.

4. ***Once you make a plan you need to start moving.*** For some people, this is the easiest part. Practice replacing some bad habits with new, more empowering ways of thinking and acting.

Case Study: When we know better we do better

Carol was general counsel for a large corporation. The CEO asked for my help because Carol was "socially awkward and lacked the necessary interpersonal skills to make the company's clients feel valued." Although she was a brilliant attorney, her lack of rapport with the company's most important clients often got in the way during contract negotiations.

Carol had learned early in life not to allow people to get too close to her emotionally. In fact, she put a lot of energy into building a wall around herself to keep people at a distance. She became an overachiever who was focused on her career and worked hard to keep people out of her emotional space. Carol had spent 38 years of her life pushing people away so she developed a very strong skill set for being aloof and defensive.

> *Why teach people to manage stored anger when we can help them to let go of it?*

Carol was so good at managing her system of defenses that she was in her third marriage and had a reputation as the "Ice Queen" in the company. Most of the people at her job avoided her or minimized the amount of time they spent in her presence.

After I worked with her through the DRP™, I am proud to say that Carol made the necessary adjustments to let go of her insecurities and fear of relationships. But because she was accustomed to bullying to get her way, she lacked the ability to influence people by building rapport and engaging others. Carol had to break some old habits and learn to utilize skills she had worked so hard to avoid.

A few weeks after Carol completed the DRP™, I stopped by her office for our regular coaching session. As I signed in at the security desk, the receptionist asked me what I had done to Carol.

"What do you mean?" I asked her. "She is actually nice now," the woman told me. "I just hope it sticks!"

IT'S TIME TO GET OUT OF YOUR OWN WAY

Consider the question I posed at the beginning of this chapter: what would the world be like if we all felt comfortable making the daily choices that lead to meaningful lives? It is time to stop running the same ineffective programs in your head and making the same dumb choices over and over.

This book is about interrupting ineffective ways of thinking and limiting belief systems so that you can act in constructive and empowering ways.

A RADICALLY DIFFERENT APPROACH

We cannot change what has happened in the past; however, we can change how we feel about it. Until recently, the approach in mental health circles has been to help the patient or client recognize his or her feelings and develop coping mechanisms. Anger management classes are an example of this approach. Students in these classes learn to recognize anger trigger points and control their behavior in order to behave in a manner appropriate to the situation. While this is a valid approach to *managing* behavior, I take the opinion that it would be a better use of everyone's time—

and the client's money—to help release the stored anger. We should not invest time and energy helping people manage harmful stored emotions when we can simply help them to let go.

The model for personal change presented in this book represents a radical departure from the traditional thinking in psychology, my field of training. This approach is different from most of the currently used approaches to personal change. The **Decision Reframing Process™ (DRP™)** model is one that I developed over the years based on the work of researchers in cognitive psychology, child psychology, Neurolinguistic Programming (NLP), leadership studies, and years of personal coaching experience.

BETTER CHOICES is not just the title of this book. It is also a goal for you and everyone who invest the time to read and complete the exercises. Your life is built on every decision you have made until this very moment. Your future will be designed by the decisions that you make starting now. When you see life through a lens of optimism and confidence, the choices you make at every moment align with your desire for meaning and fulfillment in your life.

Remember the short list of names I asked about at the beginning of the chapter concerning the people you know who are genuinely happy and perfectly content with their lives? Are you ready to add your name to that list?

CHAPTER 2

EVERYWHERE YOU GO THERE YOU ARE

Sonja was sitting on the window seat engrossed in observing the activity outside. "What are you looking at?" her grandmother asked.

"Butch and Chenille are playing ball. I was just watching," Sonja replied with a sigh.

"Why don't you go out and join them?" Grandma Mabel suggested.

"Oh no!" Sonja said emphatically. "No way. There are too many mosquitoes out there! I'm afraid of mosquitoes, Grandma. In fact, she continued, "if I was the President, I would send the mosquito truck across the country to spray everyday and get rid of all those pests!"

"Wow. That's quite a fear you have going there," Mabel responded. "Do you see that little bird sitting on the branch of that tree? I'm sure she would be so surprised to learn that you don't feel the same way about those 'pests' as she does." Mabel pointed to the bird. "She thinks the mosquitoes are yummy."

Sonja said, "It doesn't matter. I will stay right where I am—inside. I can watch them play from here."
"I'm curious. Have you ever been tackled by a mosquito?" Mabel asked Sonja with a knowing smile.

"Very funny, Grandma. I'm not going out there." Sonja said.

"What would happen if you did go out there?" Mabel asked Sonja.

"I would get bitten," Sonja replied.
"And then what would happen?" Grandma Mabel persisted.

Sonja said, "I'd have a bump."

"What is the problem with that?" her Grandmother questioned.

"The last time I had a mosquito bump, it itched for three days, Grandma!"

"What else could happen while you are outside?" Mabel asked her.

"I'd play ball with Butch and Chenille. That would be a lot of fun," Sonja answered with a smile.

"So what is more important to you, having fun with Butch and Chenille or not getting a bump?"

"I guess getting a bump isn't really that bad, is it Grandma?"

Mabel pointed out several scars on her own arms and legs. "I've had worse things happen to me and I'm still here. You could think of it this way," she said. "If you get a bump, every time it itches, let it remind you of how much fun you had with Butch and Chenille!"

Sonja started to put on her sandals. "Where are you going?" Her grandmother asked.

"I think I'll go outside for a few minutes and hang out with Butch and Chenille," Sonja said as she walked toward the door.

"Excellent!" Mabel was pleased with her granddaughter's change of mind.

GRANDMA MABEL'S WISDOM

Mabel understood many things about the way Sonja was feeling. First, Sonja was allowing a past experience with a tiny insect to keep her from doing something she really wanted to do. Her irrational fear was so consuming that she was willing to kill all the mosquitoes to accommodate it. (Insect lovers might hope she never becomes President!)

Mabel was able to help Sonja compare her feelings about getting bitten by a mosquito to the fun she would have with Butch and Chenille. This allowed her to reframe her perspective and to make a rational decision. Sonja moved past her fear about going out to play in a mosquito infested yard. What are the mosquitoes in your life?

You learned in the last chapter that people view life each day through their own set of lenses. Your perspective about issues helps you decide whether the glass is half empty or half full, whether the unknown is mysterious and frightening, or if the future is inviting and full of possibilities. From this point on, we will discuss your lenses and your perspective as the *frame* that shapes how you view the world and your place in it.

Your *frame* is constructed of mental pictures, scripts, and stories from your past. Your frame also contains how you felt about the events and the meaning you gave to the situations. You use this frame as a filter to make choices and decide what you think is appropriate behavior in any given setting.

You can not change what has happened in the past. However, you can change how you *feel* about it. When you clear out any stored negative emotions from past events, you can **reframe** the basis of your decisions so that you make better choices for yourself.

MAKING THE FRAME

Where do our frames come from? Your frame of the world did not just show up one day. Your frame has been developing all your life. Let's take an example to illustrate this point.

Imagine there was a little boy by the name of Jack whose brother chased him with a rubber snake when they were growing up.

Event = Jack's brother chases him with a rubber snake.

If Jack was being chased, that means he was running from his brother. Jack's running from his brother probably means he was afraid of either the snake or of his brother—or maybe both. So he had some **emotions** or feelings about the event. His brother's chasing him with the rubber snake made him feel afraid and possibly angry.

Event → *Feelings*

Jack's brother chases him with a rubber snake → **Jack feels fear and anger**

What do you think will go through Jack's mind the next time he sees his brother walking toward him with his hands in his pocket and a mischievous look on his face? More than likely, Jack will remember the fear from being chased by the snake. He might also think of how angry he got when his brother chased him. He has allowed the rubber snake incident to *frame* his future interactions with his brother and his feelings about snakes. The process is described in Figure 1.

Figure 1: How Frames Are Formed

Event →	Emotions→	Frame
Jack is being chased by his brother with a rubber snake	*Jack feels fear and anger*	Jack links the event with the feelings and draws the conclusion that gives meaning to his world--- 1. *Jack thinks his brother is a jerk who tries to hurt him every chance he gets.* 2. *Jack is afraid of snakes*

FRAMES BRING MEANING TO YOUR WORLD

When you woke up this morning, how did you know to be *you* in your body? When you looked into the mirror, what made you recognize the face staring back at you? Seriously consider the latter question for a moment. Other than saying, "I just did," what could you give as an answer to that question?

Who you are today, how you feel about yourself, and how you think you fit into the world are based on the accumulation of all of the memories and experiences of your entire life. These experiences form your frame of the world. It is only through your frame that you are able to define who you are today and make sense of the world around you.

> **FRAME:** *Mental pictures, scripts, and stories from your past that shape how you view the world and your place in it.*

Here is a simple way to understand this idea. If you are sitting to read this book, I'd like you to recall your actions before you chose to sit down. Perhaps you looked around for a place to get comfortable and you noticed the chair where you are now sitting. Before you actually made the decision to sit, you had to already know some things about the concept of "chair" from your past experiences. There were some simple, yet necessary things that you already needed to know that might have included:

1. How to sit in it: feet on the floor, back to the chair's back, and rear end in the seat.

2. Trust that the chair was sturdy enough to hold you. Maybe you sat in that same chair before. You knew that in the past it held you so it is likely to hold you again.

3. Remembering that the chair was comfortable in the past so it will be a good place to sit and read right now.

Maybe you are in a place where you have never been, or you do not have any previous experience with the chair where you are sitting now. Before you sat sown, did you need to ask yourself what is this object and what do I do with it?

Suppose you were beamed to earth, just now, from a place where there are no chairs or no concepts similar to "chair." How would you know what to do with the object you are now sitting in? We can only make choices by filtering current information through our past experiences.

In a similar fashion, your frame does not only define how you see the world. It also defines how you see other people. We can never really see the people around us as they really are. We see the person and judge them based on our past experiences. All we can see is our past projections of them or our past experiences with someone that they remind us of!

YOUR CHOICES GET FILTERED THROUGH YOUR FRAMES

Every decision you make goes through an assembly line of experiences, feelings, and meaning before you get to the point of acting—or not acting. For example, imagine you are in a meeting and there is something you would like to add to the conversation. What goes through your mind? Maybe the last time you spoke out in the meeting no one listened to your idea, or perhaps you even got cut off at the knees. Does your past experience make you hesitant to speak up now?

Take another example. Let's imagine you were in a loving and trusting relationship that ended because the person hurt you very badly. How likely is it that you will be willing to make yourself vulnerable to the next person that shows a romantic interest in you? Even though you realize you are cheating yourself and being unfair to the other person, you may decide that you will never love that deeply again.. The process is illustrated in Figure 2.

Figure 2: Frames influence your choices

Event →	Emotions→	Frame→	Decisions→	Actions
What happened	The feelings you had at the time	You link the event and the feelings and draw conclusions that give meaning to your world	Based on your past experience, you make choices about what you should do in current and future situations.	You think or act in certain ways based on your decisions

Let's go back to Jack and his brother with the rubber snake. Imagine that some time after the chasing incident Jack notices his brother walking toward him with that mischievous look. He decides what he should do by choosing among a series of alternatives. Jack could run before his brother has a chance to get close. He could take a pre-emptive strike and punch his brother. Or he could say to his brother, "Stop right there. Don't come any closer." Which alternative do you think Jack might choose? Do you think he will recognize that he has several alternative responses to his brother's approach? Jack will probably act out of the recognition of what he thinks his choices are.

STORED NEGATIVE EMOTIONS CAN BIAS YOUR FILTER

Let's return to the Grandma Mabel metaphor of the previous chapter. Sonja's sunglasses represent all the stored resentment, hostility, anxiety, self-doubt, guilt, and hurt you may be carrying around from your past. How you react to circumstances and the choices you make about your life are then influenced by those emotions. When Sonja believed it was about to rain, she made the decision to cut her walk short and return home. When she took off the sunglasses, she realized the day was bright and sunny with plenty of time to continue her walk with Mabel.

Frames are necessary and useful ways of filtering all the millions of bits of information that bombard you at every moment. However, you need to be able to recognize when you are allowing your actions to be influenced inappropriately by stored negative emotions from past events.

The Decision Reframing Process™ described in the next chapter offers a way to clear out stored negative emotions that no longer serve a useful purpose.

Let's summarize what you have learned so far:

1. Past experiences and how you feel about them help you frame your model of the world. They form the story of who you are and inform the choices you make about how you should act.

2. Even though the event is long over, you may be holding on to stored negative emotions and limiting decisions related to past experiences in your life.

3. These negative emotions and limiting decisions influence your daily choices and may cause your feelings to be out of proportion or inappropriate to the situation.

4. You can not change what has happened in the past. However, you can change how you *feel* about and react to past events.

5. The Decision Reframing Process™ that begins in the next chapter will allow you to clear out the stored feelings and make better, more empowered choices in every situation.

CHAPTER 3

LEARNING TO LET IT GO

Sonja had become frustrated while studying for her spelling test. She walked into the room where her grandmother was busy cooking dinner to ask for her help. As Sonja approached Mabel she heard her singing softly to herself...

> *"La, la, la, la, la, la, la, la*
> *Your dreams will never come about,*
> *If you don't live your life from the inside out,*
> *Let go of the fear and lose the doubt*
> *and live your life from the inside out.*
> *La, la, la, la, la, la, la, la."*

"What are you singing, Grandma?" Sonja asked.

"Oh just a little tune I made up many years ago. What you got there, little girl?" Mabel noticed the paper in Sonja's hand.

"Will you help me study for my spelling test? I can't seem to remember how to spell this word. I keep getting it wrong." Sonja showed Mabel the paper with the word.

"Per-snick-a-ty." Mabel sounded out the word.

"Yes," said Sonja. "It means overly attentive to detail and trivia."

"You're absolutely right," Mabel said. "It also means what your Aunt Jean is—snobbish in terms of choice and, thus, wanting or accepting only the finest things."

"Be nice, Grandma," Sonja said, giving Mabel a disapproving look.

"I'm always nice, Sonja. But whether or not I'm nice has nothing to do with your Aunt Jean being per-snick-a-ty. Here, let me show you a way to remember how to spell that word."

Mabel took out a clean sheet of paper and wrote the word persnickety in large letters on the page. She placed the paper on the counter in front of Sonja. "Close your eyes and think of how good it felt to get an 'A' on your last spelling test."

Sonja closed her eyes. When Mabel noticed her smiling, she said, "Okay, open your eyes and look at the word while you keep the feelings."

"Good," Mabel said when Sonja opened her eyes and looked at the paper.

"Now move your eyes up and to the left and picture the word big and bold and in your favorite color." Sonja obeyed. "Okay, now spell the word you see," Mabel continued.

"P-e-r-s-n-i-c-k-e-t-y." Sonja sounded out each letter.

Mabel put a clean sheet of paper in front of Sonja. "Great, now write the word on the paper here," Mabel instructed Sonja, handing her a pencil.

Sonja wrote the word without any spellings errors. Mabel flipped the paper over to the blank back side and said, "Okay, smart girl, look up and to your left again, picture the word and write it backwards on this side of the paper. Sonja got the picture of the word and confidently spelled out 'y-t-e-k-c-i-n-s-r-e-p.'

"Excellent," Mabel said hugging Sonja. "Your brain can do some pretty amazing things if you know how what to ask of it."

"You are a good teacher, Grandma," Sonja said. "But your song could use a little work."

"What do you mean?" Mabel asked Sonja. "I like my song just fine. Letting go of fear and doubt is important because they are dream killers."

"I'm not questioning the concept Grandma. It's the artistry that needs some work. You couldn't come up with any lyrics that were more creative than la, la, la, la, la"?

Mabel laughed. "I guess in addition to teaching you a new spelling strategy, I also taught you how to be a smart aleck."

"Yes, and you did a good job," Sonja responded.

GRANDMA MABEL'S WISDOM

There are two messages in this conversation with Mabel and Sonja. First, your brain is capable of doing some amazing things if you learn how to tap into the wealth of resources you have naturally hardwired within you. If you observe good spellers at work, you will see their eyes moving up to the left to access their visual memory. Then they look down to feel if it's right, or they will write the word down to access their kinesthetic channel. They then look up again to check if it looks right. Good spellers nearly always go through the same strategy - they look up or straight ahead as they spell, visualizing the word as they spell it. This is because spelling is a visual process – we need to visualize or see a word we've seen before in order to spell it.[4]

Mabel understood that we can all use the way our brains naturally work to make amazing changes in the way we learn. In order to "live life from the inside out," Mabel believed you can call upon your inner resources to let go of fear and doubt. To Mabel, these negative emotions were dream killers.

Second, Mabel makes the point that fear and doubt can be dream killers. Your emotions serve you in ways that keep you healthy and powerful. There are times, however, when you allow your emotions to work against you in ways that are unhealthy. By examining the 10 behavior types in Chapter 1, you learned to recognize how stored negative emotions can influence the way people act. This happens most often when we store emotions from memories long after the event is over and done. The emotions become part of your frame of the world.

---

[4]*According to Neurolinguistic Programming (**NLP**), ability with spelling is a function of the structure of the internal cognitive strategy you use as you spell. Thus, if people experience difficulty with spelling, it is not because they are stupid, lazy, or learning disabled but rather because they are trying to use an ineffective mental program.*

In this chapter, you will learn the process for accessing your memory storage system (an amazing way that your mind works) so that you can clear out the feelings from past experiences that may not be assisting you today.

Why Do We Resist Letting Go? -- Sarah's Story

Some people resist releasing negative emotions. They use reasoning that is as irrational as the fear, anger or guilt they refuse to release. Early in my coaching career, I offered to help a client named Sarah release her fear of snakes. She frequently had dreams about snakes and was so afraid of the reptile that she would leave the room if one appeared on the television. Despite her overwhelming fears of snakes, Sarah told me thanks, but no thanks and turned down my offer of help. She wanted to hang on to her fear.

I have to admit that, as a relatively new coach, my feelings were a little bruised at first. But she explained that she didn't want to *not* be afraid of snakes because she might not run if she saw one in her yard! Her reasoning seemed perfectly logical to her.

I asked Sarah if she was afraid of cars. When she told me she was not, I asked her if she would have enough sense to step out of the street if she saw a speeding car coming toward her! I also asked her if she was afraid of the stove on which she cooked her meals. "Of course not," she replied. "But you do know that if you touch it when it is hot, you will get burned," I warned her.

Sarah understood my point which was this: there is a difference between fear and judgment. Relinquishing your fear does not mean giving up your ability to make appropriate decisions about how to act in a given situation.

You may be comfortable with your anger or your guilt because you don't know any other way to feel. Trust me. Feelings of peace, joy, security and love are far better replacements for fear, anger, mistrust, bitterness or whatever negative emotion that you may have made your constant companion. Getting to peace and joy as your steady state requires that you learn to lose your attachment to negative stored emotions. You will not lose your ability to experience those emotions in the future. You will be wiser and exercise better judgment at the appropriate times when the negative emotions do not get in your way.

ACCESSING STORED BAGGAGE

Can you recall anything about your first year of school? Maybe it was kindergarten or first grade. Think about a specific memory. The name of your school, perhaps? What your teacher looked like? Where you lived? Can you recall anything about that first year? If you are having a difficult time recalling a memory for kindergarten or the first grade, perhaps you can recall the earliest of any of your school memories. Put the book down, now, and recall a specific memory.

Excellent! You accessed your storage system and called up a memory from your past. When was the last time that you actually thought about that memory? Where was the memory before you recalled it?

Try another simple exercise with me. Think about a situation in your past that was so funny that you laughed out loud. Maybe you had a gut wrenching laugh that made your sides hurt. Can you remember such a time? Was it a scene in a movie, a joke or something someone said or did? As you remember this time, I'll bet you are smiling, right now. Put the book down—just for a few seconds—and remember. (Note: If you carry around a great deal of sadness you may have a difficult time recalling a lighthearted moment. This will change after you complete Chapter 6 which will allow you to let go of those heavy feelings).

Now, think of a time in your past when you were angry. Remember a time when someone said or did something that made you angry. See what you saw at the time and feel what you felt at the time. Are you still smiling? Probably not. But stick with me. I am going somewhere with this.

Finally, think of a time when you were extremely excited. Maybe you were eager to go on vacation or to see someone you care about. Or perhaps you had just purchased your new car or were about to move into your new home. See what you saw at the time and feel what you felt. Are you smiling again?

What just happened? First you were laughing and then you were angry. Then you were smiling again. How did you do that? What did you do to go from joy to anger to excitement? Actually, you just changed your mind, didn't you? What a powerful thing the mind is! Did you notice that changing what you were thinking changed your feelings. Isn't that amazing?

You are about to begin the process of tapping into those stored memories and emotions to clear out any negative feelings that are impacting you today. Before we proceed with the DRP™, you should be aware of five important points related to how your mind stores your memories and feelings.

1. We will call the part of your mind that retrieved the memories about your early school years your *unconscious mind*. In this context, we will define your unconscious mind as simply that part of your mind processes of which you are unaware. Your unconscious mind has a large and complex job description. Among the many things it does for you, it is currently breathing, beating your heart, and digesting the last meal you ate. It also has the job of storing your memories and managing your emotions.

2. I am often told by people, "I have a terrible memory!" Actually, we all have excellent systems for storing all of our memories. Some people may find it a challenge to access those memories. Although you may not be able to readily recall a memory with your conscious mind, the unconscious part of you has made a recording of all of the events of your existence. Since the beginning of your time, you've had this

organic camcorder recording all the events of your life. Everything you have ever experienced, known, or felt is recorded and stored inside of you. If you were there and did, said, or felt anything, it is recorded in your memory file.

As a result of the years of accumulated memories, you have this storehouse that you carry around with you each day. You may think that you can't remember some things from your past. This belief may be true for your conscious mind.

> *Your unconscious mind is breathing for you, beating your heart, and digesting the last meal you ate. It also has the job of storing your memories and managing your emotions.*

Nevertheless, the memory is stored in your library of memories and you can have access to it. We will call this storage system your *timeline*. It has been part of the work of your unconscious mind to arrange and store memories in your timeline since you came into being.

3. In each case when I asked you to recall a memory, you went inside yourself, accessed your storage system, and came up with information about past events. You recalled a time when you were laughing, a time when you were sad, and a time when you were excited. You went to the appropriate place in your timeline where these memories were stored and your unconscious mind called up the memory for you.

Did you notice that the information had two components? For the sake of this explanation let's use a file folder as our metaphor. Imagine you opened a folder—a memory folder from your file. And there in the folder was the memory of when you were excited. On one side of the folder were the facts about what happened in that situation. On the other side are the feelings about the experience. So if you were excited about getting a new car, perhaps you opened that memory folder and recalled the specifics of the day and thought—"oh yea, here is how I felt about it!" You can not only recall what happened, but you can also experience the feelings associated with those memories all over again.

4. At this point, the skeptics, often those with the most prominent fears and limiting beliefs, begin to step to the back of the line. Some people resist releasing negative emotions. You may be comfortable with your fear, anger, or your guilt because you don't know any other way to feel. If you are skeptical at this point, you may be asking, "Do I really need to worry about past emotions because, after all, they are in the past?" My answer is simple. No, you shouldn't worry about them. Just let them go.

THE PROGRAM FOR LETTING IT GO

Each moment provides you with an opportunity to make a choice based on the present facts. When you carry around stored negative emotions, they accompany you and serve as filters for your decisions. Unresolved emotions from your past may distract you or inhibit your ability to make decisions appropriate to here and now.

The goal of the Decision Reframing Program™ (DRP™) is to allow you to let go of your attachments to the feelings associated with the memories from your past so you can address the issues of the current moment with an appropriate level of wisdom and feeling.

Recall the model illustrating how your frames are established. Look at Figure 3.1. An event occurs and you experience feelings related to the event. You now have a memory which is like a mental recording of the situation. That memory consists of three parts— what happened (the facts), how you felt about it (the emotions), and the learnings (the meaning you gave to the event). In the DRP™ you will keep the memory and the learnings from that event. The learnings and insight will serve you in the future. However, you will let go of the negative emotions that are stored along with these memories from your past.

You will use the companion CD as you work through Chapters 4-8. The CD will guide you through the release of specific stored negative emotions in each chapter. Beginning in Chapter 4, you will release anger, resentment, and hostility. In Chapter 5, you will then clear out stored sadness, depression, hurt, disappointment and grief. Chapter 6 targets fear, insecurities, and anxiety. Self-blame, shame, and guilt are addressed in Chapter 7. In Chapter 8 you will let go of limiting beliefs, self-doubt, and the decisions you have made that minimize the definition of who you really are and what you are capable of accomplishing in life.

Figure 3.1 How the DRP™ Works

	Let go of the stored negative emotion and keep the learnings		

Event →	*Emotions*→	*Frame*→	*Decisions*→	*Actions*
What happened	*The feelings you had at the time (anger sadness, fear, guilt, or a limiting decision)*	*You link the event and the feelings and draw conclusions that give meaning to your world—your story*	*Based on your past experience, you make choices about what you should do in current and future situations.*	*You think or act in certain ways based on your decisions*

Memory=record of what happened, how you felt, and the learnings

After clearing out the emotional barriers from the past, you will decide what you want for your future and use the SMART Goals tool to create a roadmap for going forward. Here are some pointers to remember:

1. It is important that you complete the chapters in order. You will release emotions in the order presented in the model: anger, sadness, fear, guilt, and limiting decisions.

2. Work in a space that is quiet and where you will not be interrupted.

3. Be open and honest with yourself. Trust your unconscious mind, and give yourself permission to go ahead and let go of any stored negative emotions.

4. You will not be required to relive painful memories. The DRP™ is a content-free process. The process is unlike traditional therapeutic and counseling techniques where you are required to discuss the details and circumstances of past events and relive the feelings. The DRP™ works with the mechanical manner in which your brain stores memories. If you are familiar with the use of computers, you may recall that if you want to delete the contents of a folder, all that is necessary is that you highlight the folder and hit the delete button. You don't have to open the folder on your computer and read the contents in order to delete them. You are smarter than a computer. Did you know that? You will let go of the stored negative emotions from past memories without having to open the folders and relive any uncomfortable emotions from the memories.

5. You are in complete control. You can stop the tape and the process at any time.

6. Trust yourself to be able to do all of this. Your brain can do some amazing things if you let it.

7. Use the work spaces in the book to write down your feelings, lessons learned, and future goals.

8. Do not listen to the tapes while driving.

9. You can repeat the process as often as necessary.

From this point on, you will to use the CD companions. Place the CD1 in your player or in your computer before you proceed to Chapter 4. When you are prompted with " *Start the CD*," begin at Track #1 of Better Choices Companion CD1.

PART II

CLEARING SPACE FOR BETTER CHOICES

CHAPTER 4

LETTING GO OF ANGER, HOSTILITY AND RESENTMENT

"Who was that man that you were talking to in the yard just now?" Sonja asked her grandmother as she came through the front door.

"Oh, that was just Mr. Kelly, our neighbor." Mabel replied.

"Why haven't I ever seen him before? Did he just move here?" Sonja asked.

"Oh no," replied Grandma Mabel. "You have never seen him because he doesn't come out much since his accident. You see, he was involved in a head-on collision with a truck. The other driver had worked a double shift and fell asleep at the wheel. Mr. Kelly is suing the trucker driver's company for his pain and suffering, so he can't appear to be too active or healthy."

"When was the accident?" Sonja wondered.

Mabel thought for a few seconds. "I guess it's been about 4 years now."

"Wow!" said Sonja. "That's a long time to stay in the house. I hope he gets paid a lot of money."

"He may or he may not. Whatever he gets can not make up for the four years of his life that he has traded. He is a bitter and miserable man. He is in a lot of pain because he won't go to the doctor unless the insurance company pays for it. His wife said they are in deep debt because of what they have had to pay the lawyers," Mabel explained.

"I wonder what they will do with the money if they win," Sonja said.

"Ms. Kelly said that they want a new house and they want to travel. They think the settlement is an opportunity to get enough money to do that," Mabel explained.

"That's really sad, Grandma. Sounds like Mr. Kelly needs to just let it go."

"Sonja, you are so right!" Mabel was shaking her head from side to side. *"It is too bad he does not understand that he has the power to do for himself the very things that he is waiting on the insurance company to do for him. He should forgive and move on."*

"But it's so hard to forgive, Grandma!" Sonja chimed in. *"Do you remember when my friend Hailey came over on Christmas day and she broke the present you had given me? I am still angry at her for that! Every time I see her my blood pressure goes up and I break out in a cold sweat. Some things you just can't forgive."*

"Does Hailey know that you feel this way?" Mabel asked her granddaughter.

"No. She just acts like nothing happened." Sonja replied.

"So who are you hurting by carrying this anger around? Is your present any less broken because you are still angry with your friend? If you do not forgive her, you have lost your present, your friend, your peace of mind, and maybe even your health. Anger rots your bones, you know."

"As usual, Grandma, you are right," Sonja sighed. *"I guess Mr. Kelly and I have a lot to learn about letting go."*

GRANDMA MABEL'S WISDOM

Mabel's neighbor, Mr. Kelly, provides a lesson for all of us in why it is important to forgive and move on. Mr. Kelly was the victim of an accident. He believed that because the truck driver was at fault, the driver's company should pay him for his pain and suffering. In our society, insurance companies don't just hand over large settlements without a fight, even though we may think this is unfair. The fighting process, however, has robbed Mr. Kelly of his power to control and enjoy his life. As long as he is waiting on the outcome of his fight with the insurance company, he thinks of himself as a victim waiting to be made whole by the courts. His anger makes him feel justified in this process.

Sonja understood that letting go of the anger and forgiving are not always easy tasks. Like Sonja and Mr. Kelly, you probably have had situations in your life where you responded with anger. You may still be holding on to the resentment and some bitterness.

In this chapter you will have a direct experience with my Decision Reframing Process™ (DRP™). You will use the Companion CD and allow yourself to be guided through the process of letting go of anger and anger related emotions. Not only will letting go take you one step closer to having peace-of-mind, it may also improve your health!

USING YOUR WHOLE BRAIN

You have probably heard it said that most people use only about 10% of their brain capacity. If that is true, it is only because no one ever taught them how to tap into the very smartest parts of themselves. We cannot change the events of the past. However, if we know the secret, we can change how we feel about and give meaning to past events in our lives. We can also clear out any negative emotions from past events that may form the basis of current and future decision making. Today, you will learn some of the amazing things your brain is capable of doing!

 ## WORKING WITH THE COMPANION CDS

In order to complete this section of the book, you need to make sure several conditions are in place.

1. First, get to a quiet place where you will not be interrupted during the six phases of the DRP™ .
2. Have the CD player close so that you can start and stop as directed during the process.
3. Have your book handy so you can write your responses during the process.

4. Finally, remember that you are in control. At every moment of this process, the choices are yours, you can be safe, and you are in control.

 *Start the Companion CD now. (CD1, Track 1) Listen to Tracks 1-5*

NOTICING HOW YOU STORE TIME (CD1, TRACK 5)

Where is the past and where is the future? Your **"Time Line"** is how you unconsciously store your memories or how you unconsciously know the difference between a memory from the past and a projection of the future. Your Time Line is your collection of memories that help you know how to be you! This concept is explained in more detail on the CD.

In relation to the space around your body, where is your Time Line?

I think of my past as *(example: behind me or to the left)*

_____

I think of my future as *(example: in front of me or to the right)*

_____

 *Start CD1 at Track 6*

Imagine you can leave your body sitting in your chair and float[5] high above to notice how you store your past and future memories. As if looking down on the top of your head, notice your timeline. What did you notice about how you store your past and future memories?

_____

_____

  Start the CD at Track 8

What to Release

During this DRP™ process you will systematically release from your Time Line all of the following stored negative emotions:

(Note: It is important to complete the program and release the emotions in this order.)

✓ **anger** (hostility, resentment, bitterness)
✓ **sadness** (grief, disappointment, depression, heartbreak)
✓ **fear** (insecurity, worry, nervousness, anxiety)
✓ **guilt** (shame, self-blame, regret)
✓ **limiting decisions** (limiting beliefs, self doubt, feelings of inadequacy)

These emotions are attached to your memories and make up the emotional events from your past. During the DRP™ , you will release each of these specific emotions from the *first event* in your Time Line. Releasing the stored emotions from the first event allows you to clear out the negative emotions

_____

[5] *Floating can be a sound, like sounds floating on the wind, or a feeling like floating in a hot air balloon.*

49

from all subsequent events easily —all the way up to the current moment.

THE ROOT CAUSE—THE KNOT ON THE STRING OF BEADS

You might be wondering what effect the first event of anger has on your life today—particularly if that event happened so long ago that it may seem small and insignificant from your adult perspective today. Let's use a string of beads as an analogy to illustrate why the first event is important.

Think of each bead on the string as an Emotional Event in your life. An Emotional Event is an experience (or experiences) that create an emotional meaning—a story you tell yourself– which affects you in later life.

> **An Emotional Event**
>
> *is an experience (or experiences) that create an emotional meaning—a story you tell yourself– which affects you in later life.*

tell yourself– which affects you in later life. That emotional meaning could be positive (enjoying *show-and-tell* time as a kid leads to enjoying public speaking as an adult) or it could be negative (*show-and-tell* time as a kid leads to hating public speaking as an adult).

An event often becomes a **Significant** Emotional Event if it is an intense experience—something traumatic which creates great emotional power. The younger you are, the more difficult it is to deal with that emotional power.

For example if you are forty years old and your parents decide to divorce, you may be angry and disappointed. But if you are five years old when they decide to divorce you may be devastated. Children do not have available to them the full array of thought processes that an adult has. As a result, the child draws different conclusions about the meaning of an event than an adult draws.

The child may create a story about her role in the divorce—maybe blaming herself for Daddy leaving—and she may decide when she grows up that she will not give herself completely in a relationship because her partner will leave her.

The child creates this story with beliefs that do not reflect the reality of the situation. Then she makes decisions throughout the rest of her life that are filtered through the story. And so it happens that you create your story and then your story creates you.

DESCRIBING THE DRP™ MODEL (CD1, TRACKS 8-10)

The goals of the Decision Reframing Process™ (DRP™) are for you to 1) let go of stored negative feelings associated with the memories from your past, beginning with the *root cause* memory, 2) get the lesson from those events in a way that you can use the learnings in the future, and 3) complete the forgiveness process.

The Decision Reframing Process™ Model
(The Balloon Process™)

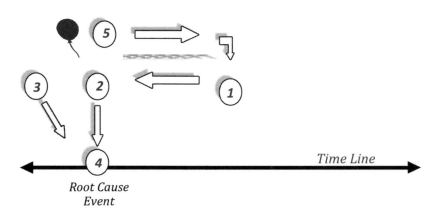

Root Cause
Event

Past   **Now**   **Future**

The Process

1 = *above now, face the past*
2 = *high above the root cause event, let go of the balloon*
3 = *check your feelings*

4 = *get the learnings and forgive*
5 = *notice the rearrangement all the way back to now*

Get the Lesson and the Learnings

Getting the lesson means making the appropriate observations and really understanding the meaning of the event. Learning in this way allows you to use the insight as you make choices in the future. The importance of the learnings should not be understated. Getting the lesson allows you to quickly release the emotion and use the learning to assist you in the future. Think of the lesson as a cloth to wipe your negative emotions clean.

An Opportunity to Forgive

Ordinary forgiveness is letting bygones be bygones - letting go of the past while still holding onto the idea that something wrong or bad happened[6]. That often seems like a difficult task, and it usually takes a very long time before we begin to feel the forgiveness.

With the DRP™, the release is more total since it involves a shift in perception that allows you to learn a valuable life lesson from the situation. The learnings are experienced as a profound insight and will simply come to you in an instant. When you receive this insight, you can let go of being a victim and find peace, even in the most unpleasant of situations or memories of what happened.

---

[6] For more information about forgiveness, I recommend *Radical Forgiveness, Making Room for the Miracle* by *Colin Tipping.*

We will begin the process by clearing out all stored anger. Anger is an intense emotion. There are very few people on earth who have not, at some point in their life, been disappointed, misled, deceived, or injured by someone else. The memory of the harm leaves a festering wound that strips you of your power and creativity. Here are some points to remember about anger:

1. Anger is a natural defense mechanism intended to keep you from being abused when your boundaries have been violated or you believe you have been wronged. It allows you to stand up for yourself in the face of danger.

2. When you let go of stored anger from your past memories, you will not give up your ability to get angry in the future. You will continue to be able to experience anger when appropriate and in the context of the present moment.

3. You may have different labels for anger or those feelings closely related to anger. These labels may include resentment, bitterness, and hostility. Rage is an intense level of anger.

    > *Anger and resentment are not meant to be stored and carried around like baggage.*

4. Letting go of anger and resentment is not for the benefit of the other person. It is for you. Unless you release the stored anger from the past memory, you allow yourself to become a continuing victim to the person or situation.

5. Anger and resentment are *disposable* emotions. Experience them. Learn from them as they relate to a specific situation or event. Then you can discard them because they have no more use for you.

I feel angry about (*CD1, TRACK S 8-12*)

_____

_____

 *Start CD 1 at Track 13*

(Note: The following questions refer to all anger you may have stored. They are directed at your unconscious mind and work to loosen your model of the world related to the stored emotion. It is important that you answer each question.)

What *would* happen if I *did* let go of this anger?
(This question allows you to visualize your life without the anger.)

_____

What *wouldn't* happen if I *did* let go of this anger?
(This question brings out the secondary gains. It helps identify the benefits of holding on to the anger that might be lost once you let go. Reflect upon this question carefully and honestly.).

_____

What *would* happen if I *didn't* let go of this anger?
(This question will bring out the pain or costs of holding on to the anger and provide motivation for letting it go.)

_____

What *wouldn't* happen if I *didn't* let go of this anger?
(This question confuses the left brain and gets you beyond the conscious mind. It can make you aware of the values and inner forces that were hidden. It is best to answer the question intuitively rather than logically.)

_____

 Start CD 1 at Track 14

Root Cause for the first event of anger---When?

_____

Start CD 1 at Track 15 --Clearing out the anger

NOW WHAT?

Now, look back at what you wrote on page 53, in the section, "I feel angry about." How have your feelings changed? *(CD1 Track 16)*

Most of the time, people are able to release the anger from past events in one try. You may notice that thinking about this event does not generate the same feelings as before. If you still have some negative feelings, take the time to examine those feelings closely. You will probably realize that what you are experiencing may be one of the emotions we have not yet released, like hurt or guilt.

Occasionally, some negative emotions remain, so you may need to repeat the process. Be patient with yourself. Before you repeat the process for anger, work through Chapters 5-8 and complete the processes for the releasing the other emotions. You will have the chance to check back on your feelings about this memory after you have released sadness, fear, guilt and limiting decisions.

Now, I feel...

_____

What were the learnings about anger from the root cause memory in position 4? (CD1 Tracks 16-17)

_____

_____

Will you apply your learnings daily, weekly, or monthly?

_____

(Read the opening pages of Chapter 5. Then start CD1 at Track 18 when prompted.)

CHAPTER 5

RELEASING STORED SADNESS

Mabel walked into the room and noticed Sonja slumped down in the chair. The curtains were drawn, making the room dark, even though it was the middle of the afternoon.

"Hey, little princess. How ya doing?" Mabel asked her.

"Fine." Sonja answered solemnly.

"You don't look so 'fine' right now," Mabel said. "How are you really doing?"

"I'm having a bad day, Grandma. Rippy died." Sonja's eyes grew teary.

"Your puppy? I'm so sorry, baby," Mabel said sympathetically. She sat down next to her granddaughter. "I have an idea. Go get your swimsuit and we'll go to the pool for a little while."

"No thanks, Grandma. I don't feel like going to the pool today. Besides, my swimsuit got bleached in the wash and it doesn't look good anymore. I think I have grown and it doesn't fit me anymore, either. On top of that, I still have this poison ivy rash on my leg and it doesn't look good. Life sucks right now Grandma," Sonja whined.

"You want some cheese with that whine?" Mabel teased Sonja. "You slipped right into a pity party. Sorry, little girl. I understand that you are sad about Rippy, but I don't attend pity parties."

Mabel took off her sandal and showed it to Sonja. The heel had been chewed.

"What happened to your shoe?" Sonja asked.

"Rippy happened to it," Mabel said. "That dog chewed anything that would fit in his mouth. From my rocking chair on the front porch to the water hose in the back yard, I have never seen a dog with such peculiar habits."

"Did you ever see him chase his tail?" Sonja asked. She started to laugh as she told Mabel about the time Rippy was so busy going in circles chasing his tail he didn't notice when he

got to the edge of the front porch, and he just fell right off into the flower bed!"

"I'll bet that was a sight!" Mabel said. She and Sonja were both laughing as they remembered Rippy's silly antics. "Look what I got for you." Mabel interrupted the laughter.

Opening the bag she had brought in with her, Mabel held up a brand new, red swimsuit. "The last time we went swimming, I noticed that you were getting a little leggy for your old suit. So I bought this one for you".

"My favorite color!" Sonja said excitedly. "I can't wait to put it on. I can be ready for the pool in five minutes, Grandma," Sonja called back over her shoulder as she left the room to get ready.

Mabel smiled, thinking to herself, "That was easy!"

GRANDMA MABEL'S WISDOM

Sonja was sad about the death of her puppy, Rippy. Like anger, sadness is a normal emotion. Feeling sad every once in a while is natural. However, when you are sad, the body's ability to feel, think, move, and even digest is literally depressed. The world seems dark and unfriendly. You have a hurt deep inside that crushes your heart and your spirit. Life seems to sit on you like a 500 pound weight.

When Mabel recognized Sonja's emotional state, she attempted to lift her out of her mood by offering a trip to the pool. But Sonja was committed to feeling bad. Not only did she turn down a trip to do something she really enjoyed, she began a downward spiral into deeper levels of sadness. Feeling sorry for herself, Sonja started to point out all the things around her—like the bleached swimsuit that didn't fit any more and her case of poison ivy—to support her sadness.

When Mabel focused Sonja's attention on Rippy's funny antics, Sonja's mood shifted and she laughed. Once Sonja felt better, she was able to do something enjoyable again. Mabel understood that breaking the grip the sadness had on her granddaughter was critical.

The sources of our sadness can be many and varied, from heart break and disappointment to grief and loss. Some people make a distinction between sadness and the medical condition known as "clinical depression." We will not address those differences in this context.

YOUR SADNESS CAN AFFECT THOSE AROUND YOU

Severe reactions to loss may carry over into familial relations and cause trauma for children, spouses, and any other family members. For example, there is an increased risk of marital breakup following the death of a child, or a 'faith crisis' may occur as bereaved persons reassess personal definitions of their faith and trust in God.

> *When you are sad, life seems to sit on you like a 500 pound weight.*

Like other stored emotions, sadness can be released from your past memories. It is just as important to release stored sadness as it is anger, fear, guilt and limiting beliefs. People often report feeling "lighter" after releasing the burden of sadness they have been carrying around.

 Start CD 1 at Track 18

Root Cause for the first event of sadness---When? *(CD 1 Track 19)* _____

A NOTE ABOUT GRIEF (CD1 TRACK 20)

It is natural to feel a sense of loss when persons we care about are no longer with us. We miss them and the role they played in our lives. However, some people confuse grief with memories. Some people believe that letting go of the grief surrounding the loss of a loved one is the same as letting go of their memory. In fact, just the opposite is true. Grief and pain from the loss can mask joy and the love from the relationship. When it is not painful to recall the memory of someone we love, we are more likely to spend time thinking about the person. We can recall the joyful moments and smile as we think of them. Joy and gratitude for the shared times are much better legacies to leave behind for the grieving loved ones than pain and suffering. Don't you agree?

WHAT MAKES YOU SAD? (CD 1 TRACK 21)

Think about your life. Can you identify at least one source of sadness? Make a note to yourself in the space below. Just as we did with the exercise releasing anger, we will check back and notice how your feelings have changed about this situation once you have cleared out all stored sadness.

I feel sad about...

_____

_____

Note: The following questions refer to all sadness you may have stored. They may seem a little awkward to you, but they are directed at your unconscious mind and work to loosen your model of the world related to the stored emotion. It is important that you answer each question.

What *would* happen if I *did* let go of this sadness?

_____

What *wouldn't* happen if I *did* let go of this sadness?

_____

What *would* happen if I *didn't* let go of this sadness?

_____

What *wouldn't* happen if I *didn't* let go of this sadness?

_____

 Start CD1 at Track 22—Releasing Sadness

NOW WHAT? (CD1 TRACK 23)

Now, look back at what you wrote on the previous page in the section, "*I feel sad about.*" How have your feelings changed?

Now, I feel...

_____

What were the learnings about sadness from the root cause memory at position 4?

_____

_____

Will you apply your lesson daily, weekly, or monthly?

_____

(Read the following section and the opening pages of Chapter 6. Start CD1 at Track 24 when prompted)

Most of the time, people are able to release the sadness from past events in one try. You may notice that thinking about this event does not generate the same feelings as before. If you still have some negative feelings, take the time to examine those feelings closely. You will probably realize that what you are experiencing may be one of the emotions we have not yet released, like fear or guilt.

Occasionally, some negative emotions remain, so you may need to repeat the process. Be patient with yourself and wait to repeat the process until after you have completed Chapters 6-8.

CHAPTER 6

RELEASING STORED FEAR

"Twelve dead in school shooting" Sonja read the headlines of the paper that reported the unfortunate incident resulting in the death of her classmates. She and Mabel talked as they drove to the memorial service for her friends.

"Grandma, why did Steven kill those people? " Sonja asked. *"He didn't even know them."*

"It is because he was afraid," Mabel explained.

"Afraid?" Sonja asked. *"Everyone is saying Steven was angry because he said someone disrespected him. He said some kids called him a freak. Everyone was afraid of him. Why would you say he was afraid?"*

"Sonja, what do you think? Why would the fact that other people disrespected Steven make him want to kill them? Why would he care?" Mabel asked.

"I don't know," Sonja said. *"They called him a freak. I guess he cared because it was important to him to be respected. Maybe he wanted everyone to think he was important,"* Sonja speculated. *"Let me guess what you are going to say here,"* she continued. *"You are going to tell me that sticks and stones can break my bones but names can never hurt me and that Steven shouldn't have let the people who called him names push his buttons. Right?"* Sonja was proud of herself for understanding the deeper meaning of the situation without Mabel having to point it out.

"That's a pretty insightful observation, little girl!" Mabel was pleased with her granddaughter's growing wisdom. *"Actually, you might be surprised to learn that names and labels can hurt, Sonja—but only if you give them that power. People can only insult you with your permission,"* Mabel said. *"Let's think about this for a moment. What is the big deal about those kids calling Steven a freak? Suppose they really*

didn't like or respect Steven," Mabel replied. "Why is that a problem?"

"Maybe he didn't like the feeling of being rejected, Grandma. I guess he needed those kids to like him. He might have felt that if people didn't respect him, they could just do whatever they wanted to him? I suppose he thought bringing the gun to school and killing those people would make others think he is tough and they would give him more respect? " Sonja sighed.

"Fear has many faces, Sonja. Do you think Steven was afraid that other people had the power to take what he thought was his--respect? Or maybe, deep down inside he feared they were right and he really did think of himself as a freak— whatever that means to you guys these days. Maybe he was actually afraid that he did not have control over what happens to him. We may never really know what form of fear motivated Steven's decision to kill those people," Mabel explained to Sonja.

"Fear is the cause of many things that we do and do not do in life. What would have happened if Steven didn't care what other people thought of him? What would have happened if he knew that he was in control of his life and no matter what other people said he was still worthy of being respected because he respected himself?"

"My friends might still be alive," Sonja realized sadly.

"Exactly," Mabel said.

GRANDMA MABEL'S WISDOM

Mabel understood that fear can take on many forms. Often those who hurt others do so because they are afraid. They mask their fear by acting tough or by not allowing others to get close to them. Persons who are secure and confident do not allow themselves to be inappropriately affected by the opinions of others and have no need to prove themselves or to cause harm to others. They can make choices about their life based on their confidence, their joy, their passions, and their talents. In the absence of this confidence, people may act and make choices out of their insecurities.

WHAT IS FEAR?

Fear is actually a healthy and necessary emotion. It is a normal human response to an external threat. You are hardwired with a mechanism that protects you in the presence of a situation when you need to feel fear. The *"fight or flight"* response" is your body's primitive, automatic, inborn response that prepares the body to "fight" or "flee" from perceived attack, harm, or threat to your survival.

When your fight or flight response is activated, you experience sequences of nerve cell firing, and chemicals like adrenaline, noradrenalin, and cortisol are released into your bloodstream. These patterns of nerve cell firings and chemical releases cause your body to undergo a series of very dramatic changes.

> **When your *"fight or flight"* system is activated, you tend to perceive everything and everyone in your environment as a possible threat to your survival.**

When your fight or flight system is activated, you tend to perceive everything and everyone in your environment as a possible threat to your survival. You scan and search your environment "looking for the enemy." Your respiratory rate increases. Blood is shunted away from your digestive tract and directed into your muscles and limbs which require extra energy and fuel for running and fighting. Your pupils dilate, your awareness intensifies, your sight sharpens, impulses quicken, and your perception of pain diminishes. Your immune system mobilizes with increased activation and you become prepared—physically and psychologically—for fight or flight.

By its very nature, the fight or flight system bypasses your rational mind where your reason, logic, and better thought out beliefs exist. You are literally "dumbed down" when you are in flight or fight survival mode. Your thinking is distorted. This state of alert causes you to perceive almost everything in your world as a possible threat to your survival. You see everything through the filter of possible danger. You narrow your focus to those things that can harm you. Fear becomes the lens through which you see the world. As such, you tend to see everyone and everything as a possible enemy.

FEAR IS A DREAM KILLER

Our fight or flight response is designed to protect us from the proverbial saber tooth tigers that once lurked in the woods and fields around us, threatening our physical survival. When we face very real dangers to our physical survival, the fight or flight response is critical and automatic.

Today, however, most of the *saber tooth tigers* we encounter are not a real threat to our physical survival. Today's saber tooth tigers consist of rush hour traffic, missing a deadline, bouncing a check or having an argument with our boss or spouse. Nonetheless, these modern day threats trigger the activation of our fight or flight system as if our physical survival is threatened. On a daily basis, toxic stress hormones flow into our bodies for events that pose no real threat to our physical survival.

Because we are focused on short-term survival, making clear choices and recognizing the consequences of those choices are difficult. We lose the ability to relax and enjoy the moment, and we live from crisis to crisis with no relief in sight.

It is almost impossible to cultivate positive attitudes and beliefs when we are stuck in survival mode. Our heart is not open to positive outcomes and possibilities, and our rational mind is disengaged.

STORING FEAR

Some people are afraid of things that are easy to identify. Snakes, insects, and heights are examples of these kinds of fears. Other fears take on a form that is not so obvious and may be triggered by the absence of something that provides safety and security.

Examples of these fears may include fear of the loss of a job, loss of love or a relationship, or loss of control. Other fears include the fear of rejection, fear of being alone, fear of engaging other people, fear of death, fear of failure, or fear of success. The list can go on. In either case, at some point in your life, your decision to become afraid of any of these targets of fear is attached to a memory from your past. You have framed your current model of the world from stored memories related to these fears.

In Chapter 2 you learned how *frames* are formed. Recall this example:

Jack's brother chases him with a rubber snake →Jack feels fear and anger

In all probability, in the future Jack will tell himself the story that he is afraid of snakes (and maybe his brother). As a result, when he encounters a snake, he will feel fear. Even if he is not physically threatened in that situation, the stored fear from his past memory will be triggered. His body will create the same neural and chemical responses that would be present if a snake physically threatened him.

FEAR CAN SHUT YOU DOWN

Fear associated with past memories can interfere with our ability to react realistically and effectively to a current situation. We run from a situation when we are afraid, an act of which may be literal in that we actually move our bodies out of the way. Or, we may run away from a situation by withdrawing emotionally.

In the opening story of Chapter 2, Sonja is afraid of getting bitten by a mosquito. Her fear prevents her from doing something she really would enjoy doing—hanging out with Butch and Chenille. She could see the place she wanted to be, but her fear kept her inside the house.

What are the mosquitoes in your life? The mosquitoes represent fear barriers that get in the way of choices that lead to joy, peace, and fulfillment in your life. If you are feeling powerless, fear is a root cause. If you have ever longed to commit yourself to something and felt disappointed that you have never achieved that goal, take a good look at why you have never allowed yourself to go ahead. Is fear the cause?

> **Are you stuck in a job or relationship? Maybe you have a strong desire to make another choice but you can't bring yourself to take the first step.**

Are you stuck in a job or relationship? Maybe you have a strong desire to make another choice but you can't bring yourself to take the first step. What you may be experiencing is fear. People often are affected by the fear of change, the fear of not changing, fear of the future, fear of taking a chance, fear of intimacy, fear of being alone, fear of letting people know what you need or who you are, fear of flying, gaining weight, fear of germs, taking tests, driving a car, talking, performing in public, fear of flying, fear of growing old, fear of snakes, fear of social settings, fear of failure, fear of success, etc. You may even fear letting go of the fear from your past memories!

How many times *this week* has fear prevented you from doing something that you really wanted to do?

FEAR CAN MAKE US ACT INAPPROPRIATELY

On the one hand, fear can shut us down and keep us stuck. On the other hand, fear can also cause us to act defensively, in inappropriate ways, and do things that we should not do. Have you ever found yourself doing something absolutely ridiculous or inconsistent with the way you normally act because you are afraid of losing something or someone? Fear causes us to lie, steal and hurt other people. Jealousy, a fear-based emotion, is fueled by this type of fear. Think of the silly or even dangerous things that some people may do because they fear being on the losing end of a love relationship.

LET GO OF THE FEAR

What does peace feel like? You have done an exquisite job of clearing out stored negative emotions up to this point. You might even feel lighter because you have let go of the heaviness of the stored anger and sadness. Now you are about to release the stored fear by letting go of every decision you have made in the past to fear an object, person, or even a situation. [7]

You will still have the ability to be afraid in the future. Your flight-or-fight response will not go away. However, your future choices will not be filtered through a frame of fear and insecurity. You will choose to act based on your knowledge, preparation, confidence, passion, and all the other positive aspects of yourself. The result will be—better choices!

◉ *Start CD 1 at Track 24*

I feel fearful about .... (CD1 Track 25)

_____

What *would* happen if I *did* let go of this fear?

_____

What *wouldn't* happen if I *did* let go of this fear?

_____

What *would* happen if I *didn't* let go of this fear?

_____

_____

[7] *If your religious tradition teaches you to "fear the Lord," this process will not change you in that respect.*

What *wouldn't* happen if I *didn't* let go of this fear?

_____

⊙ **Start CD 1 at Track 26**

Root Cause for the first event of fear---When?

_____

⊙ **Start CD 1 at Track 27—Letting go of the fear**

NOW WHAT? *(CD1 TRACK 28)*

_____

Now, look back at what you wrote earlier in the section, "I feel fearful about." How have your feelings changed?

Now, I feel...

_____

What were the learnings and lesson about fear from the root cause memory? (CD1 Track 28)

_____

_____

Will you apply your learnings daily, weekly, or monthly?

_____

(Read the next section and the opening pages of Chapter 7. Then start CD2 at Track 1 when prompted.)

Most of the time, people are able to release the fear from past events in one try. You may notice that thinking about this event does not generate the same feelings as before. If you still have some negative feelings, take the time to examine those feelings closely. You will probably realize that what you are experiencing may be one of the emotions we have not yet released, like guilt or limiting beliefs.

Remember, some negative emotions may remain and you may need to repeat the process. Be patient with yourself. Before you repeat the process for fear, work through Chapters 7 and 8. You will have the chance to check back on your feelings after you have released guilt and limiting decisions.

CHAPTER 7

RELEASING STORED GUILT

Mabel and Sonja were having dinner. "How is your salad?" Mabel asked.

"It's good, but it's also sort of like the day I had today— all mixed up!" Sonja answered.

"What happened?" Mabel inquired.

"Remember my friend Hailey?" Sonja asked.

"Is that the same Hailey who broke your toy and made you so angry?" Mabel questioned.

"Yes, that's her. But I'm not angry anymore. I let that go," Sonja explained. "Anyway, I haven't seen her in forever and today I see her three times. It was really strange."

"Go on. What happened?" Mabel asked when Sonja paused to take a few bites of her dinner. She was eager to hear about Sonja's encounter with Hailey.

"The first time I saw her, we were in the store. She must have seen me first and by the time I noticed her, she was ducking down another aisle as if to avoid bumping in to me. Then I saw her getting into the car and leaving," Sonja continued.

"A little while later, I went to the tryouts for the school play. I was running a little late so most of my classmates were already there. When I arrived, I noticed Hailey sitting and laughing with a group of other kids. When she saw me, she stopped smiling and she got up and left. She didn't even come back to the auditions. I guess she changed her mind about being in the play."

"And here's the third thing that happened," Sonja went on. "When I went to my locker at the end of the day, I found a note and a piece of candy taped to the outside. The note read, 'I'm sorry. Hailey'. I don't know what to think of this, Grandma." Sonja put her fork down and propped her elbows on the table.

"It sounds to me like your friend Hailey has a serious case of guilt. When we think we have wronged someone, it can be hard to face that person. Our decisions and actions get filtered through the feelings of guilt, and we avoid people and situations that remind us of what we think we did wrong. Hailey feels so bad that she gave up on being in the play rather than face you," Mabel explained.

"Wow! All that over a stupid toy, Grandma?" Sonja asked. "But that's such a small thing."

"Good for you! I'm glad to hear you say it is insignificant that Hailey broke your toy. If I recall correctly, you were still pretty upset about it not too long ago. Since you let go of the anger, you are able to recognize that it really was just a simple mistake." Mabel was proud of Sonja.

"I think I will help Hailey let go of her guilt, Grandma. She doesn't need to put all that energy into avoiding me and thinking I am upset with her," Sonja said.

"Excellent!" Mabel said. "I agree with your earlier observation. The salad you are eating really is like your day today. Both the salad and your experiences today nourished you and helped you to grow!"

GRANDMA MABEL'S WISDOM

A simple mistake can cause so many bad feelings, ruin relationships, and kill motivation. Sonja's friend, Hailey, was feeling guilty about the broken toy. Mabel understood that when we think we have wronged someone, facing that person can be difficult. She was proud of her granddaughter for realizing that once she let go of being upset over the broken toy, she could understand that a simple mistake was not worth the amount of energy she was giving it. It was also not worth sacrificing a friendship. Without the anger, Sonja was

Unlike anger, which can be a call to action, guilt is more often a call to inaction. Feelings of guilt can shut you down.

able to go to her friend and help her release the guilt that separated them.

FORGIVE YOURSELF, NOW

Guilt is a sentiment that you have done wrong, regardless of whether the wrong doing actually occurred. You blame yourself for not being perfect. You judge and punish yourself, and you may lose your confidence and self-respect.

Unlike anger, which can be a call to action, guilt is more often a call to inaction. Feeling guilty can lead to your becoming convinced that you are a terrible person and not capable of doing anything right. It can cause you to sit and brood. You may feel undeserving, ashamed, and hold yourself back.

Living with guilt is a painful and self-destructive experience. Guilt kills love, joy, and happiness in a relationship. Feeling guilty can lead people to drugs and alcohol, to unprotected sex, to driving drunk, to hurting the people they love, and to other destructive behaviors.

WHEN WE KNOW BETTER, WE DO BETTER

We all make mistakes. Sometimes we make *big* ones. Making mistakes is part of the human growth process. This is how we learn. Every time we make a mistake, we learn a little more about life. As a result we are wiser and more aware.

We may have been taught to believe that feeling guilty is necessary when we make a mistake. Yes, if we break a rule that society holds dear, our conscience would most likely act on us. We will likely feel remorse. This feeling of remorse is a helpful guide for avoiding behavior which takes us out of harmony with nature and other people. But when we have made a mistake, it is important to distinguish between disapproving of ourselves and disapproving of what we did. We are not what we sometimes do.

Think back to a time when you made a mistake. Notice that at the time, you had a particular state of mind and a particular way of seeing life. You acted out of your state of mind—how you understood the world to be and how you saw yourself in the world. From that state of mind, your actions were totally consistent with how you thought and approached life at that moment. You used the information and knowledge available to you and made the very best decision you knew how to make.

We all go through life doing the very best we can with the limited skills and awareness that we have at a particular point in time. We do the best we can with what we have. No one wakes up in the morning and says, "*I think I'll deliberately mess up today.*"

In all likelihood, a year from now you will be much wiser than you are today. The wisdom you will have a year from now will come as a result of living and growing. That wisdom isn't with you today because you have to learn the lessons and sometimes make the kinds of mistakes that help you grow to that wisdom.

Don't judge, condemn, or beat yourself up because you view past situations and choices through the eyes of your current wisdom. Give yourself credit for your growth.

You should also be aware that as you continue to grow as a person, in future years, you may look back on some of the choices you are now making and say to yourself, "Ouch! I don't know what I could have been thinking!"

YOU ARE NOT YOUR BEHAVIOR

You are not your behavior. When you have made a mistake, it is important to distinguish between condemning yourself and acknowledging the decision or act. We all go through life doing the very best we can with the extremely limited skills and awareness that we have at a particular point in time.

You can forgive yourself for acting out of your limited awareness and for the damage you may have caused as a result of your not knowing. Are you willing to forgive yourself for not being wiser and more aware? You can not change what has happened in the past. You can start to make more resourceful choices, beginning now. Let the guilt go. Forgive yourself.

ASSAULT SURVIVORS' SHAME AND GUILT

Although what happened to them was not their fault, many survivors experience both guilt and shame after being sexually assaulted or abused. I'd like to make a distinction between feelings of shame and the feelings of guilt. Shame is often confused with guilt, but they are not the same.

You feel guilty when you judge your behavior as wrong or as failure and you focus on what you should have done differently and what you can do to repair the damage. Survivors sometimes feel guilty because they feel they did something wrong which caused them to be assaulted or abused. They may say to themselves, *"If I wasn't wearing that dress...if only I hadn't drunk so much...I shouldn't have been alone with him, I shouldn't have made him angry,"* etc.

Sometimes other people contribute to survivors' guilt by judging and blaming them. They may blame the victim for being in the wrong place at the wrong time or for staying in a dangerous relationship. The survivor feels guilty because it seems like the action caused the assault. But it is important to remember that **the only person to blame is the person who committed the assault or abuse.**

Shame, on the other hand, is the feeling that *'I am a bad person because this happened to me'* or *'what will people think if they know I let my spouse beat up on me?'* It is the feeling that you think others are judging you or that someone will think poorly of you because of what happened.

Shame can be longer lasting and more intense than guilt. The feeling of shame can be so intense for rape and abuse victims that many never tell anyone what happened to them. Even in psychotherapeutic settings, victims of rape often avoid talking about what happened to them.

Although guilt and shame are distinct emotions, you can release them together in the same process. For the purposes of this program, you do not have to spend time analyzing and compartmentalizing your feelings. By now, you have learned to trust your unconscious mind. You know you can give yourself permission to let go of the bad feelings—no matter what the label. Your peace of mind is waiting on the other side of the time you invest in letting go. So let's get to it.

⊚ *Start the CD2 at Track 1*

I feel guilt about (CD2 Track 2)

_____ ___

What *would* happen if I *did* let go of this guilt?

_____

What *wouldn't* happen if I *did* let go of this guilt?

_____

What *would* happen if I *didn't* let go of this guilt?

_____

What *wouldn't* happen if I *didn't* let go of this guilt?

_____

⊚ *Start CD2 at Track 3*

Root Cause for the first event of guilt---When?

_____

⊚ *Start CD2 at Track 4—Letting go of Guilt*

NOW WHAT? (CD2 TRACK 5)

Now, look back at what you wrote on the previous page in the section, "*I feel guilt about.*" How have your feelings changed? Maybe you feel a sense of relief. You might feel like a burden has been lifted.

Now, I feel...

_____

What were the learnings and lesson about guilt from the root cause memory?

_____

_____

Will you apply your learnings daily, weekly, or monthly?

_____

(Read the following section and the opening pages of Chapter 8. Start CD2 at Track 6 when prompted.)

Most of the time, people are able to release the guilt from past events in one try. You may notice that thinking about this event does not generate the same feelings as before. If you still have some negative feelings, take the time to examine those feelings closely. You may realize that what you are experiencing may actually be a limiting belief.

Remember, some negative emotions may remain and you may need to repeat the process. Be patient with yourself. Before you repeat the process for guilt, work through Chapter 8 to release limiting decisions. Then you can check back on your feelings about guilt and shame.

NEW HABITS FOR THE FUTURE

In the future, get in the habit of taking responsibility and making amends rather than taking on guilt in situations where you have made a mistake. If the wrong doing is not yours, do not take on guilt for it. Do not allow yourself to feel guilty over something that was out of your control.

You will continue to make mistakes in the future. Taking responsibility for your actions will help lessen the feelings of guilt when you notice them. For example, if you make a mistake at work, instead of responding to the mistake with a guilty feeling, find a way to prevent that mistake or a similar one from happening again.

A sincere apology also goes a long way. If you feel guilty about something for which you can make amends (for example, you yelled at the kids because you had a headache or you broke a promise), simply respond to the situation and your feeling of guilt by making amends. Apologize. The other person will feel better, and so will you.

You have a choice regarding your response to any situation. Taking responsibility improves your ability to respond more appropriately in the future. Maybe you didn't make the best decisions in the past. That doesn't mean you can't start to make better choices, right now.

Start CD2 at Track 6

CHAPTER 8

LIVING SMALL---*RELEASING LIMITING BELIEFS*

Mabel hung up the phone with a little more energy than usual. She shook her head and mumbled as she headed toward the kitchen where Sonja was helping herself to a glass of juice. "How could someone with so much education make such dumbass choices?" Mabel complained.

"What's wrong?" Sonja was very surprised at her grandmother's reaction to the phone call from her friend.

"I really get annoyed when intelligent, perfectly equipped people limit themselves. My friend Mae wouldn't recognize a solution to her problems if one strolled up and bit her on her whiny little nose because of her 'I can't do this. And I can't go there!' "

"I fall into her trap every time," Mabel continued her tirade. "I find myself making recommendations to help her. Every suggestion I make, the answer is 'I would do that but...' **But** *this excuse or* **but** *that excuse. Excuses, excuses, excuses! But, but, but! She needs to get her but out of the way."*

"Wow!" At first, that was all Sonja could think to say in reaction to Mabel's passionate ranting. "Ms. Mae is so smart and beautiful. Just looking at her, you wouldn't think she was so committed to living small," Sonja finally mustered up the nerve to say. "When I grow up, I'm going to travel the world—maybe in a hot air balloon. I will sit on top of a pyramid and write a poem about sand. And I am going to hitch a hide on the space shuttle. I wonder if I can see our house from space or maybe see a whale jumping up in the ocean."

Sonja's enthusiasm shook Mabel from her soapbox. "Good for you. That sounds like a pretty exciting life," Mabel said, congratulating Sonja on her plans.

"And I'm going to build a school for children to help them learn to live LARGE!" Sonja paused and thought for a

moment. "You know, Grandma," she said pensively, "I might have to live about 120 years to get everything done."

Mabel laughed and marveled at her granddaughter. "Sounds like you have it all figured out."

"I have a question, Grandma. Is **dumbass** a bad word?"

"It is not a very nice thing for a sweet little girl to say," Mabel answered with a smile.

"So when I'm older, I can say it, right? Please be more specific, Grandma, when can I say it?" Sonja wanted to know.

"Oh...let's see...when you are my age and a perfectly capable woman annoys you with her limiting beliefs about herself and her place in the world. But not till then," Mabel said waving her finger at Sonja.

GRANDMA MABEL'S WISDOM

Mabel was annoyed because she recognized in Mae the power that Mae could not recognize in herself. Her friend noticed the limitations associated with each of Mabel's suggestions. Rather than saying to herself, "Good idea, Mabel. Let me think about what I need to do to make that happen," she created a barrier and an excuse. From her way of thinking, the *limitations* on her options in life far overshadowed the *opportunities*.

Limiting beliefs are doubts about who you are and what you are capable of doing. They are formed as a result of the messages you are taught about how the world works and how you fit into it. All of your insecurities and self-doubts are learned from others in the things they say to you and the ways that they react to what you do..

A limiting decision precedes every limiting belief you have adopted. You make the initial decision and it shapes your belief system going forward. Your choices in life are then filtered through that belief system.

Mabel could have told Sonja that her dream of sitting on top of a pyramid was silly. In that simple moment, Sonja's way of viewing the world and her place in it would have been diminished. Sonja could have made the limiting decision that her dreams were not achievable or that they were not worth pursuing.

In this section, you will let go of all the limiting decisions from your past. You will identify the self-doubt, insecurities, and limiting belief systems that keep you stuck. They will go into the balloon and—*pop!*

DEEP DOWN, YOU DON'T THINK YOU CAN

In an earlier chapter, I asked you to make a list of the people that you would categorize as *loving their life*. As you probably realized, that list is not very long. Why is that?

Limiting beliefs can keep you from experiencing the full range of choices you really have. You don't experience these options because you don't believe they exist for you. It would surprise you to recognize how your limiting thinking may have permeated your everyday life and how it may show up in some simple ways.

The summer before my son went off to college, he convinced the family to take a trip to Disney World as a sort of *"good-bye-to-my-childhood-hello-college-student"* activity. Experiencing theme parks naturally means going on the roller coaster rides. However, when it came to roller coasters, my husband had the designated assignment to ride with the kids while I took the pictures from solid ground.

On this particular trip, my son reasoned that this was the last time for me to ride with "my little boy" and that he wanted me to accompany him on *The Mummy*. I found myself giving the usual excuse, "No, I don't do roller coasters."

As soon as the words rolled off my tongue, the DRP™ voice in my head asked, *"So, when did you decide that?"* I recognized the limiting decision I had made and so did my family. They wouldn't let me off the hook. As we stood in line to enter the ride, I closed my eyes, went back on my timeline, and found the original decision.[8] Evidently, I made that choice when visiting Six Flags over Georgia as a little girl. I had previously let go of my fear of roller coasters but evidently I held on to the limiting decision.

I let go of the decision right there in line, got on the ride with my family, and enjoyed it immensely. The picture we purchased shows the ride plunging at break neck speed down a ridiculously steep slope and me grinning from ear to ear with shear delight! My early decision had caused me to miss out on a lot of fun in the past—but not in the future!

LETTING OTHERS DEFINE YOU

What you learned in kindergarten is true—you are only as good as you expect to be. This is not necessarily a problem unless much of the way you and others define you is based on negative stereotypes. A *stereotype* is a characteristic or set of characteristics that is attributed to all the members of a class or group. Members of the class are labeled and are assumed to act or think in a certain way because they belong to that particular group. We all have stereotyped others and maybe ourselves.

Stereotypes often form the basis of prejudices and are usually used to explain real or imaginary differences due to race, gender, religion, age, ethnicity, socio-economic class, disability, and occupation among the many groups to which you may belong. Can you think of at least one stereotype for each of the following groups of people?

---

8 After completing the DRP™, you will also have the necessary tools to address your limiting beliefs and decisions when they show up in the future.

- Blonds
- Senior citizens
- Computer
  Programmers

- Asian students
- Baptists
- Football players

Think of the different ways you can label yourself. Now think of the expectations that our society holds for each of your labels. Because of the labels you carry, society holds specific expectations that can either empower or limit you if you internalize them.

There is a theory that has gained influence among behavioral scientists that some members of stigmatized groups expect themselves to do worse when faced with stressful situations like taking a test or rising above a barrier. The self-fulfilling prophecy[9] actually comes true because they internalize the expectation. One study even found that when older individuals had internalized stereotypes about hearing loss their hearing actually got worse![10]

As a child, you learned from the adults around you and from other children how to define yourself and how to think of your value to society. Most of the ways you have learned to judge yourself as right, wrong, good, or bad comes from someone else's opinion of you. This works in both positive and negative ways. If you were encouraged and affirmed as a person who possessed talents and characteristics that were valued, you naturally see yourself in that light later in life. But if others had low expectations for you, frequently

---

[9] *A **self-fulfilling prophecy** is a prediction that directly or indirectly causes itself to become true due to feedback between belief and behavior. (i.e. I believe I will get a cold and I start to sneeze and get the sniffles as a result.)*

[10] *Becca R. Levy, Martin D. Slade, and Thomas M. Gill, **Hearing Decline Predicted by Elders' Stereotypes**, The Journals of Gerontology Series B: Psychological Sciences and Social Sciences 61:P82-P87 (2006)*

criticized you, and pointed out your flaws, it would take a very concentrated effort on your part to grow your self-esteem beyond that programming.

LIMITING BELIEFS AND LIMITING DECISIONS SHOW UP IN YOUR SELF-TALK

If you find yourself thinking about something you want or dreaming about something you want to do and your dream ends with "but," you have just been stopped by your limiting belief. Limiting beliefs and limiting decisions show up in your self-talk. Have you ever had any of the following thoughts?

> *Most of us hide behind a wall of "buts" everyday. Behind these excuses lie all of the self-doubt and insecurities that you have been programmed to believe.*

I can be happy. .. I can be prosperous... I can be healthy...

My life can be more fulfilling *but...*

BUT ...Family responsibilities take all of my time and energy.
BUT ...This is all life has in store for me.
BUT ...I don't know how.
BUT ...I don't have enough education.
BUT ...I don't have enough money.
BUT ...I'm too old.
BUT ...I'm not old enough.
BUT ...I don't have anyone to keep the kids.
BUT ...I don't have a husband/wife/spouse.
BUT ...I don't have but 10 years until I can retire.
BUT ...I need a steady paycheck.
BUT ...It is too late to follow my dreams.
BUT ...I am expected to do what I am doing.
BUT ...I don't see myself like that.
BUT ...I don't have time to exercise.
BUT ...I have been disappointed too many times in the past.
BUT ...This is the way I've always lived. I can't change.
BUT ...I'm not good enough.

BUT ... I'm not smart enough.
BUT ... My family/friends would criticize me.

Most of us hide behind a wall of "buts" everyday. Behind each *but* is a powerful limiting belief. Behind these excuses lie all of the self-doubt and insecurities that you have been programmed to believe. Here is the key. These limiting beliefs are so powerful only because *you give them power*. You allow them to be barriers that stop you dead in your tracks rather than motivating factors that cause you to create a plan and work around the barrier. Rather than inviting you to look at the situation as a call to action, "but" statements keep you from acting.

It's time to love the skin you are in, tear down the wall of buts and learn to grab hold of the life you want to live.

GETTING YOUR "BUT" OUT OF THE WAY

Limiting decisions and limiting beliefs restrict your choices and your capacity to change in positive directions. "But" statements stem from these limiting beliefs and are evidence of the belief system behind the statement. "But" statements represent only one form of evidence that a limiting belief is operating. In the following sentences, limiting beliefs are stated in negative terms—that is, in terms of what the person believes can't or won't happen.

"The American dream is not for me."
"People don't like me."
"I can't do math."
"I am not as aggressive as other leaders."

Or, your limiting beliefs can be stated in terms of what you think you should do or what will happen. For example:

"I will turn out just like my mother or father."
"I have to please everyone." or "Everyone has to like me."

"I will get sick and then I can get attention."

Can you think of others? In either case, negatively stated or positively stated, at some point in life a decision was made about what could or couldn't be done. The belief system grew from that decision. As a result, the way you speak about your world reflects how expect challenges and barriers to overwhelm possibilities and opportunities in your life.

⊚ *Start CD2 at Track 7*

Limiting Decisions I have made *(CD2 Track 8)*

_____

_____

What *would* happen if I *did* let go of all limiting decisions?

_____

What *wouldn't* happen if I *did* let go of all limiting decisions?

_____

What *would* happen if I *didn't* let go of all limiting decisions?

_____

What *wouldn't* happen if I *didn't* let go of all limiting decisions?

_____

⊚ *Start CD 2 at Track 9*

Root Cause for limiting decisions---When? (CD2 Track 9)

_____

⊚ *Start CD 2 at Track 10 –Letting go of Limiting Decisions and Self-doubt*

People are usually able to release most limiting decisions from past events in one try. However, unlike some of the previous stored negative emotions, limiting beliefs may require several trips on your timeline. As you go through your daily life, you will recognize when a limiting belief emerges. It will show up in your self-talk. When you find yourself saying "I don't" or "I can't," you can then use the CD to go back and find the limiting decision that occurred and release it. This is what I did with my decision about riding roller coasters.

Now, look back at what you wrote on the previous page, "Limiting decisions I have made." How have your feelings changed? At this point, you may recognize some of the opportunities you have passed up in the past. Your current understanding will give you the new attitude to make different choices in the future. Your choices will be based on a feeling of confidence about what you are capable of doing rather than on self-doubt and small thinking.

Now, I feel... (Record how you are currently feeling about yourself)

_____

What were the learnings about limiting decisions from the root cause memory at position 4?

_____

Read the following sections and Chapter 9. Then start CD2 at Track 11 when prompted at the end of Chapter 9.

MAKING SURE YOU GOT IT ALL (CD2 TRACK 10)

You have cleared out stored anger, sadness, fear, and guilt in earlier sections of the book. Flip back to the pages in each chapter where you recorded "*I feel angry about (Chapter 4), I feel sad about (Chapter 5), and I feel fearful of (Chapter 6)*".

Carefully examine your feelings about what you wrote in each section and record your feelings below.

I released the anger. Now, I feel...

_____

I released the sadness. Now, I feel...

_____

I released the fear. Now, I feel...

_____

I released the guilt. Now, I feel...

_____

If you find there are some lingering emotions at this point, it is because you did not release all of the feelings. Make a list below of any residual feelings and the situations to which they are attached.

Feeling   Event

_____ _____
_____ _____
_____ _____
_____ _____
_____ _____
_____ _____

After you have completed the list, answer the following set of questions for each remaining situation that was not cleared.

What *would* happen if I did let go of the _____ *(feeling)*?

_____

What *wouldn't* happen if I did let go the _____ *(feeling)*?

_____

What *would* happen if I *didn't* let go of the _____ *(feeling)*?

_____

What *wouldn't* happen if I *didn't* let go of the _____ *(feeling)*?

_____

How do I benefit from holding on to _____ *(feeling)*?

_____

After you are completely congruent with releasing the stored negative feelings, work through the appropriate chapter(s) (Chapters 4-8) again. You can repeat this cycle for as many times as it takes to clear out all stored negative emotions. You can also use this process to clear emotions from situations as they occur in the future.

PART III

Living with Peace and Confidence

CHAPTER 9

PEACE OF MIND

Done with her meal, Mabel stood up from the dinner table and announced to Sonja, "I'll wash the dishes and you dry. Ok?"

"Let's do it," Sonja said reluctantly.

"How was the first day at camp?" Mabel asked Sonja as she handed her the casserole dish that she had just washed. "Did you enjoy it?"

"Not all good, Grandma," Sonja responded, her mood suddenly dampened. "The food is great—especially the brownies. The kids are nice and I like the camp counselors. But when we play games, I feel like a real geek. I can't do that cool Double-Dutch jump rope thing like the other girls," Sonja went on to explain. "They can do cart wheels and one girl can even hula hoop for 5 straight minutes. I even struck out every time it was my turn at bat!"

"Excellent!" Mabel said with excitement as she held her arms out inviting Sonja to come close for a hug.

"Excellent? Why is everything always so excellent to you, Grandma? It's either excellent, or fantastic or great! Why is that? Can't life just suck sometime?" Sonja was annoyed with her grandmother.

"I suppose it can—for some people." Mabel hugged Sonja and then gently pushed her out to arms length. "But not for me," she continued. "Listen. The fact that your friends at camp can do all sorts of cool things means you have lots of different ways to learn. You can learn from the camp counselors and you can learn from your friends. I think that is excellent! You will be a bad mamma jamma come August!"

Sonja laughed at her grandmother as she circled her hip, imitating a hula hoop move.

"You see, Sonja," Mabel continued, "whether a person recognizes the down side or the up side to a situation is all a matter of perspective. If you have a positive perspective on life, you can notice the excellent side of every event. You know—the silver lining in every cloud or the glass half-full. But if you have a pessimistic perspective, the first thing you notice in any situation is the problem. The perspective you take will determine whether you get any joy and meaning out of a situation."

"I was following you, Grandma, but you just lost me," Sonja said. "What do you mean?"

"Fantastic!" Mabel said.

Rolling her eyes, Sonja mumbled under her breath, "Oh, here we go again."

Mabel laughed. "A few minutes ago you complained that the other kids in camp knew more cool games than you, right?"

"Yes," Sonja answered, "but after you pointed out that I can learn from my friends and know how to double-Dutch and cart wheel and all the other cool stuff just like them, I started to feel excited."

"Exactly, you get the point! You changed your perspective on the situation and that changed your feelings. Now you don't see a problem. You see an opportunity!"

"Grandma, you are absolutely brilliant!" Sonja said.

"I know darling," Mabel answered. "Aren't you glad you inherited my genes?"

"Oh yes, I am a bad mamma jamma!" Sonja and Mabel laughed as they went arm-in-arm into the house.

GRANDMA MABEL'S WISDOM

In this story, Mabel skillfully reframed her granddaughter's perspective about the situation at camp. Sonja's original attitude led her to think of her friends' skills and knowledge as a problem. When Mabel helped her to see the situation from a different perspective, Sonja could recognize the opportunity to learn from her friends and she got excited. The situation didn't change. Sonja's perspective changed.

In the opening story of "Chapter 1," Mabel and Sonja were looking at the same sky as they walked in the woods. But they drew different conclusions. When Sonja viewed the day through her dark sunglasses, she was convinced that the rain was coming and that she and her grandmother should head for home to avoid the bad weather. Having a very different perspective of the day, Mabel advised Sonja to remove the shades and recognize that the day was just lovely.

Everyone views life and the circumstances of each day through his or her own set of lenses. Your perspective about issues helps you decide whether the glass is half empty or half full or whether the unknown is inviting and full of possibilities rather than mysterious and frightening. Like Sonja, you have the powerful ability to change your lens and your perspective.

BREAKING BAD HABITS

Now that you have released the anger, sadness, fear, guilt, and limiting decisions, you may need to also let go of some bad habits of making decisions based on that old stuff. You decide whether a situation is a problem or whether it holds exciting possibilities by the attitude you take as you think about it. Before you completed "Chapters 4-8" of this book, you filtered the circumstances of each current event through the lenses of stored negative emotions from the past. Decisions filtered through those negative emotions can be pessimistic, defensive, or hostile. Chances are you have developed some habits or routine scripts that you have used in the past when dealing with people or situations.

Now you are different. From this point on, you may find yourself having an old fearful thought and realize that you no longer feel the same way about that situation. You may have been in the habit of speaking about how you *used to* feel. Maybe you have said things like "*I don't do roller coasters.*" If you really stop to think about roller coasters now, you may be willing to give them a try!

Here is a simple test. If you let go of the grief about the death of someone you cared about, try thinking of a happy memory with that person. As you think of the happy time, I'll bet you begin to smile. *Smiling* when you think of the person is the new habit you will embrace and exhibit from now on. Expecting to *feel sad* when you think of them is the old habit that you will eliminate.

CHARACTERS IN MABEL'S FAMILY-REVISITED

In reading "Chapter 1," you encountered the characters in Mabel's family. Their actions and choices were filtered through lens of stored negative emotions. Following is a review of the characteristics of the personality types presented in that chapter and some suggestions for breaking the bad habits that accompany each personality type. If you had previously been in the habit of acting in any of the following ways, you may use the four-week journal in "Chapter 11" to monitor your growth and your changes in perspective. Be patient with yourself and give yourself credit for every successful step you take.

The Rut Dweller

Old Bad habit: Rut-dwellers see themselves as stuck. They know exactly what they want but they can't seem to get started making their dreams a reality.

New Habit: Having let go of fear and limiting decisions, you are no longer afraid to make a move. Make a list of possible alternatives for your future, pick one, map out your plan, and then get moving to make it happen. You will use the SMART goals tool in the next chapter to start you on this new path.

The Touchy-Defensive

Old Bad habit: Touchy defensives are defensive and argumentative. They take feedback as a personal attack.

New Habit: Your defensiveness came from insecurity and self-doubt. Now and in the future you can laugh at yourself, admit when you are wrong, and learn from your mistakes. Catch yourself when you start to perceive comments from others as personal attacks. Record your observations in the 4-week journal in Chapter 11.

The Bully

Old Bad habit: Like a bully, you may have been mean spirited, angry, controlling and abusive in the past.

New Habit: You have released the hurt and anger from your past and you have forgiven yourself for behaving badly. Now you are in a position to examine the relationship you have with each person in your life, beginning with your immediate family. Make sincere apologies, where necessary, and commit to help and empower others rather than abuse and tear them down.

The Broken Hearted

Old Bad habit: Because life hurts, you may have given up all together, turning to drugs and other means of medicating the pain away.

New Habit: Without the pain, you have new energy and new options. Use the learnings to start over and move ahead. You will use the SMART goals tool in the next chapter to start you on this new path.

The Diva

Old Bad habit: In the past, you put a great emphasis on dressing up on the outside to deceive the world and hide a fragile sense of self on the inside.

New Habit: The way you define yourself is no longer based on limiting beliefs and self-doubt. You do not have the need to shout and convince others how wonderful you are. You can be patient, go about your business with confidence, and wait for the world to notice—*or not.* In the future, observe how comfortable you are with not having to be the center of attention.

The Door Mat

Old Bad habit: You have suppressed who you are and put aside your desires and feelings to give in to what others want.

New Habit: You now know that your needs and desires have as much value as anyone else's. The world needs what you have to offer. With your new confidence, you can be honest with yourself about what you want and don't want in your life. You can establish boundaries and speak up when they are violated. This is not the same thing as being a selfish person. Make a list of the new ways you would like to behave in the future. Commit to yourself to be true to who you are.

The Victim

Old Bad habit: As a victim, you blamed, pointed fingers, and hid behind excuses rather than take responsibility for your actions or for your life.

New Habit: You now recognize that *you are driving your bus.* You are **at cause**. Your new call to action is *"What am I going to do about this?"*

The Wet Blanket

Old Bad habit: Your focus was on the negative outcome in any situation. You could always identify the worst case scenario and that became your reality.

New Habit: When faced with a situation, you now tell yourself "this is excellent." Then you ask yourself, "What good thing could happen here?"

The Aloof

Old Bad habit: You may have resisted relationships that require you to emotionally commit or engage at any significant level.

New Habit: You have released the fear of people getting close to you. Examine your inner circle and chose one relationship. Look for opportunities to engage and make yourself more emotionally available to that person and watch what happens.

The Pre-Phoenix

Old Bad habit: Life had burned you. It may have seemed unfair that the advantages that other people enjoy were so far out of your reach.

New Habit: It's time for a rebirth. The burned old shabby feathers are gone. Now you can rise again brilliant, rejuvenated, and ready to soar. Make a plan and get moving.

SURROUND YOURSELF WITH POSITIVE PEOPLE

There is a school of thought that says if you want to know what you are really like, just look at the people around you. The people with whom you chose to associate are a reflection of you. You like being around them because they are like you.

You really are a different person than you were before you picked up this book. Your fresh perspective is motivating you to think about the new ways you want to interact with the world and the people around you. You now have the confidence to make new friends. Seek out people who find the bright side of life a great place to be.

Your challenge now is to create habits that allow you to maintain this progress. You may need someone to help you notice some of the changes. You might consider asking a close friend to point out when he notices you making statements or doing things that are a reflection of your new learnings. You might also ask them to point out when you occasionally fall back into some old habits you thought you had eliminated.

It could be that your friends are delighted to find that the *"wet blanket"* in the group is now confident, optimistic, and even more delightful to be around. Or, now that you have a different, more positive perspective on life, you may find yourself at odds with your old circle of friends. You can help them understand the new you if you learn to use phrases like *"I used to think like that, but I don't feel the same way about that situation anymore."*

SELF ACCEPTANCE-INTEGRATION MEDITATION

You have changed in many fantastic ways over the course of the last eight chapters of this book. You have cleared out negative emotions and learned to make space for peace in your life. The next section will allow you to take a few moments to integrate the changes.

 Start the CD2 at Track 12— Integration Meditation

Namaste! **(Pronounced nah-ma-stay) The perfect light in me salutes the perfect light in you.**

Read the opening sections of Chapter 10. Then start CD2 at Track 14 when prompted.

CHAPTER 10

LIVING FROM THE INSIDE OUT

Mabel stood on the steps of the front porch and watched Sonja wave goodbye to her friends on the school bus. "How was your day?" Mabel asked when she noticed Sonja's slumped shoulders.

"It was terrible, Grandma," Sonja sulked. "My teacher gave me an 'F' on my math exam. Look at this!" Sonja reached into her book bag and handed her test paper to her grandmother.

*"Ms. Brooks gave you an F?" Mabel asked, noticing all the red marks on the test. "She **gave** you an 'F' as a gift?"*

"Very funny, Grandma" Sonja said. "I wouldn't have gotten an 'F' if this woman knew how to teach. She is so boring."

"So you failed the test because the teacher is boring? There are blank spaces on your paper where answers should be, Sonja. Do you think that had anything to do with your grade?" Mabel continued her questioning.

"That geeky Jeremy sits next to me. He made wheezing noises all through the test. How was I supposed to concentrate? By the time I really got warmed up to write down my answers, the teacher was taking up the papers," Sonja whined.

"Ms. Brooks could have given me more time on the test, but she refused to help me out. And if you remember, Grandma, I didn't want to take math this semester anyway. You were the one who insisted that I sign up for it. Now look what has happened. I have an 'F' on my test." Sonja continued with her string of complaints.

"Wow! You want some cheese with that whine?" Mabel, chuckling, asked Sonja. "It seems as if the whole universe has cooperated to make sure that you flunked your math test. That's some conspiracy. What happened when you

got an '*A*,' on your literature essay last week? Was that also a gift from your teacher? Did the universe conspire to make you succeed?"

"Of course not, Grandma. I worked hard on that paper. I earned that 'A,'" Sonja insisted. She was getting irritated at her grandmother.

"Based on the amount of time I noticed you studying for the math exam, I would say that you earned that 'F' also. Would you agree?" Before Sonja could answer, Mabel continued. "Baby, you have to decide who is driving your bus, be at cause, and live your life from the inside out," she advised her granddaughter.

"Drive my bus? Be at cause? Live my life inside out? I don't know what all of that means, Grandma, but I'm sure you're going to tell me," Sonja said sarcastically.

"It all means, my sweet granddaughter," Mabel patiently explained, "that you don't give other people the power to do for you what you can do for yourself. Being at cause and driving your own bus mean that you take responsibility for the results of your actions. You don't look to blame others or hide behind excuses for what happens---like receiving an 'F' on the math exam. When you start to believe that someone else controls what happens to you, then they are driving your bus," Mabel went on. "They can take you to wherever they like because they call the shots. You just go along for the ride. Before you know it, you will be depending on others to make you happy, to keep you healthy, and to provide an income for you. You need to decide from inside of yourself how things will turn out and take responsibility for everything that happens in your life. That's living life from the inside out! Got it?"

"I got it, Grandma." Sonja had to admit that Mabel was always the voice of wisdom.

"Now, what are you planning to do about that math grade?" Mabel inquired.

"Ms. Brooks told us that we could correct our exams and get half credit for our work," Sonja explained. "I guess I'll go get started on it."

"Great! But first, give me a big hug," Mabel instructed Sonja.

Sonja playfully squeezed Mabel so tightly that she lifted her right off the ground. "'Uugghh," Mabel grunted, "if you do that again, you are really going to bring my insides out!" They locked arms and laughed as they went inside the house.

GRANDMA MABEL'S WISDOM

Sonja complained and pointed to a series of circumstances that she blamed for her grade on the math exam. She saw herself as the victim of unfortunate circumstances—from the boring Ms. Brooks to her classmate's wheezing. From Sonja's perspective, these circumstances all contributed to her failing math grade.

Mabel knew that successful people take responsibility for getting results. She was concerned that her granddaughter would continue to define herself as a victim under the control of someone or something else. She did not want Sonja to believe the power to change her circumstances was outside of herself.

Mabel wanted Sonja to understand that once she accepted total responsibility for every decision she makes and every action she takes, there is virtually nothing that she can not accomplish.

BE AT CAUSE

Can you think of times in your life when it was easier to place blame on something external rather than to accept responsibility for what happened? How did you feel as you pointed a finger of blame? I'll bet feelings of anger and resentment soon followed the blaming.

A person who does not completely accept responsibility for his or her life is subject to anger, hostility, fear, resentment, and doubt. Since you have just cleared out all of those stored emotions, let's not go there again!

In life, you either create results or you are at the effect of some cause outside of yourself. You either take responsibility for your outcomes or you blame and/or give control to others. You get to choose the side of the equation.

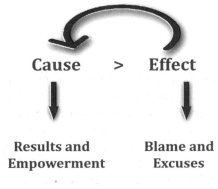

Cause   >   Effect

| Results and Empowerment | Blame and Excuses |

Which side are you on?

BE AT CAUSE!

There is a relationship between the amount of responsibility you accept and the amount of freedom you feel. The more responsibility you take, the more freedom you have to make decisions and to do the things you want to do. Your life will never be better than your ability to take responsibility for your choices and for your behavior. Before you move to the next section where you will set goals for your future, make a commitment to *be at cause* in all areas of your life.

NOW, WHAT DO YOU WANT?

"What do you want?" is not always an easy question to answer when the response is filtered through past disappointments. Setting goals is a lot easier when you can be optimistic about the future and confident about your ability to take the necessary steps to achieve your goals.

In the past you may have allowed fear, insecurities, or other unconscious behavior, habits, or limiting beliefs to sabotage achievement of your goals. Now that you have cleared the space for creating an exciting and fulfilling future, you will use two tools presented in this chapter to plan your path forward.

The tools are **Mind Mapping** and **SMART goals**. A Mind Map[11] is a powerful way of expressing the thought patterns, pictures, and associations that already exist in the brain. The mind map is a visual thinking tool which reflects the way the brain naturally thinks. It uses both sides of the brain and it harnesses the full range of cortical skills—word, image, number, logic, rhythm, color, and spatial awareness—in a single, uniquely powerful manner.

The objective of using the mind map in this context is to allow you to think through the many options you have for your life and to decide what you would like your life to look like in five years. Once you have completed your mind map, you will learn the process for putting a single goal into your future by using your timeline.

MIND MAP FOR THE NEXT FIVE YEARS

The basic learning principles of mind mapping or those of similar concepts have been around for centuries. The concepts have been used by some of the greatest creative geniuses and most influential individuals in history.

To do the Mind Mapping exercise, you will need a set of colorful markers or pencils, a blank sheet of paper (or the blank space to draw the map in your book.), your mind, and your imagination.

---

11 *The technique of Mind Mapping® was created by Tony Buzan. Learn more about this technique at http://www.buzanworld.com.*

These are the steps you will follow:

1. Draw an image to represent the central idea
2. Draw branches, using colors. Each branch gets a different color.
3. Add a word to the branch. Use one key word per branch.
4. Draw images on the branch.
5. Extend the branches and make connections. Your brain works by association. It likes to connect things together.

Let's Get Started

Step 1: Turn the page or book sideways and start at the center of the page with the central concept, "*Me in five years.*" **Draw an image that represents this central concept**. Use colors freely.

Step 2: Put your thoughts around the central idea of what you want your life to be like five years from now. **Draw a main branch for each idea.** Use different colors for each main branch. Remember to consider the different areas of your life:

- Health   • Career
- Relationships   • Family
- Spirituality   • Finances

Step 3: Make new branches from the main branch with related ideas. Write down a word or draw the first things that come up in your mind when you start to think about related issues, persons, object, and goals. You can focus on as many areas as you like or focus on one specific area.

The lines must be connected, starting from the central image. The main branches are thicker, organic, and flowing, becoming thinner as they radiate out from the center. Remember, each word, image, or idea must be alone and sitting on its own line. Make the lines the same length as the word/image.

Step 4: Keep your hand moving. If ideas slow down, draw empty lines, and watch your brain automatically find ideas to put on them, or change colors to re-energize your mind.

Think as fast as you can and come up with an explosion of ideas. Translate them in words, images, codes, or symbols. Select key words and print using upper or lower case letters.

Free associate As ideas emerge, print one or two word descriptions of the ideas on lines branching from the central focus. Allow the ideas to expand outward into branches and sub-branches. Put down all ideas without judgment or evaluation. Don't be concerned if an idea seems unrelated.

Add relationships and connections. Sometimes you see relationships and connections immediately and you can add sub-branches to a main idea. Sometimes you don't, so you just connect the ideas to the central focus. Organization can always come later; the first requirement is to get the ideas out of your head and onto the paper.

Step 5: Decide what themes or information you will use from the mind map in the next section on goal setting.

Mabel's Mind Map

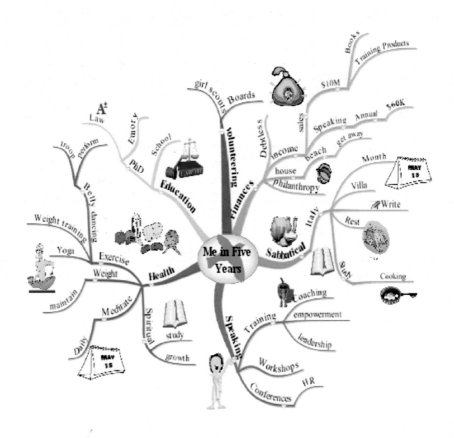

Draw your mind map on this page

Me in Five Years

A Peek into The Future

Before you move on to the next section, would you like to take a look at your life five years from now? One of the amazing things about your brain is that it will allow you to form that picture.

Sit comfortably, then stat the companion CD so that we can take a peek at your exciting future.

⊙ **Start CD2 at Track 14 –A Peek Into the Future**

Read through the sections below and begin the CD at Track 16 when prompted.

SETTING SMART GOALS

The process of setting SMART goals is common in the business world. However, the approach you will use in this context borrows from the Neurolinguistic Programming (NLP)[12] model which enables you to go beyond mere "goal setting" into the actual "programming" of your mind to drive you toward your desired outcome. Incorporating some key components will allow you to integrate the goal setting process so that it includes the neural mechanisms underlying the way you state and envision the goal. How does this work?

Your brain works primarily from your sensory system (pictures, sounds, feelings). The NLP goal setting model addresses this characteristic of the brain by forming the goal so that it is sensory specific. In addition to using the sensory system, your brain also uses word meanings that drive the sensory system. That means the way you state the goal does make a difference. For this reason, you will set

---

[12] *See **The Magic of NLP Demystified** by Tad James for more information about NLP and SMART Goals*

SMART goals that will allow your neurology and physiology to help you obtain your desired results.
SMART is an acronym for:

S	Specific and simple
M	Measurable and meaningful to you
A	Achievable and stated "as if now."
R	Realistic and responsible
T	Timed and toward what you want

SPECIFIC and SIMPLE

Goals should be straightforward, simple, specific, and emphasize what you want to happen. Make your goal as detailed as possible. Being specific helps you to focus your efforts and clearly define what you are going to do.

For example, instead of setting a goal to lose weight or be healthier, set a specific goal to lose two inches off your waistline or to walk five miles per week at an aerobically challenging pace.

MEASURABLE and MEANINGFUL TO YOU

How will you know when you have achieved your goal? What will you accept as evidence? If you set a goal of being debt free, how will you know when you are there? A possible answer to that question could be that you will know you have achieved your goal when you receive your credit card invoice and the *balances owed* box reads "$0." Get the picture?

Also, make sure you want the goal for *you.* The goal should be self-achievable. It is very important that the outcome is something you can directly influence. A goal such as "My children will show me more respect." is not a well-formed goal.

ACHIEVABLE and stated "AS IF NOW"

Your goal needs to stretch you and motivate you beyond your current situation. However, if you set goals which may be too far out of your reach, you probably won't commit to working toward achieving them. For example, a goal to lose 20 pounds in one week is probably not attainable. A goal to loose one-two pounds per week is attainable and therefore more motivating.

Stating your goal "as if now" allows you to create a picture of what it would actually be like to achieve it. As you imagine having achieved the goal, you are forced to be clear on the specific results you want. Also, by imagining you are there in the moment, you can check for alignment with your values and ensure the goal *feels* right.

REALISTIC and RESPONSIBLE

Realistic means doable. Your goal is realistic if you truly believe you have the skills and abilities to accomplish it. A goal of never again eating sweets, cakes, and chocolate may not be realistic for you if you really enjoy eating these foods.

In addition to being realistic, the goal should be responsible. A responsible goal is ecological. All the areas of your life will be affected by the achievement of your goal. Therefore, you check the "ecology" of your life and make sure the goal will benefit you in all areas. You will not achieve a goal about which you have some internal conflict. Ask yourself if you achieved your goal today, would it be okay. By doing this, you ensure that the goal is congruent and maintains balance in all areas of your home/work life.

TIMED and TOWARD what you want.

Decide on the specific time you would like to have the goal completed. Your goal can also be grounded within a specific timeframe, for example *by "May 1ˢᵗ."*

To make your goals "toward" what you want, they should be stated in positive terms. An "away goal" is stated in negative terms like "I don't want to be broke." Your goal should state what you want—not what you don't want.

Examples of SMART Goals

You can begin the SMART goals process by first thinking of what you want in general terms. Then refine the goal to meet the SMART criteria. Use the examples below to help you understand this concept.

General Goal: "I want to write a book."
SMART Goal: *"It is now Mother's day 2010 and I am giving my mother a copy of my completed book as a gift."*

General Goal: "I will make more money on my job next month."
SMART Goal: *It is now January 31, 2011. I have made $75,000 in sales with a profit of $18,000 for the month.*

General Goal: "I want to go back to school."
SMART Goal: *It is now May 2014. I am at the graduation ceremony to receive my BA degree in accounting.*

PUTTING A GOAL IN YOUR FUTURE

You may use the space below or a separate sheet of paper to write your SMART goals. Write as many goals as you like and in as many areas of your life as you like.

SMART Goal

_____

_____

SMART Goal

_____

_____

SMART Goal

_____

_____

SMART Goal

_____

_____

SMART Goal

_____

_____

Writing the goal is the first step. Now, you will set the goal.
Please remember that:

✓   It is important to set one goal at a time.
✓   The SMART goal is the one that you will set into your
    timeline.

Choose the first goal you would like to set. Then sit back
comfortably and start the companion CD.

 **Start the CD at Track 16 –Putting a Goal In Your
Future**

YOUR LIFE FROM THIS POINT FORWARD (CD2 TRACKS 16-17)

Congratulations! You are on your way. You may be feeling a
sense of excitement and confidence that is new for you. Enjoy
the new you! Use the journal in the next chapter to monitor
the changes in your life for the next four weeks.

CHAPTER 11

ONE FOOT IN FRONT OF THE OTHER

Mabel watched Sonja with quiet curiosity as her granddaughter repeatedly stared at a picture on the desk in front of her and then tilted her head back and closed her eyes. Sonja went through this cycle of studying the picture and then closing her eyes several times before she noticed her grandmother in the room.

"Hey Grandma," *she greeted Mabel sheepishly.* "I guess you are wondering what I'm doing, right?"

"Yes, I was wondering," *Mabel admitted.*

"Look at this." *Sonja handed Mabel an 8 1/2 x 11 inch canvas. The painting depicted a concrete parking lot bordered by a wooden fence. The tall buildings of the cityscape filled in the skyline behind the fence. In the center of the picture, a flower with bright yellow petals defiantly tall and straight sprouted from the concrete and stood in stark contrast to the greys and browns that made up its surroundings.*

"Mr. Cameron, our art teacher, painted this picture," *Sonja explained.* "Our homework assignment is to think of a name for it."

"That's a very nice picture. Mr. Cameron is a very talented artist. What do you plan to name it? Something like **'Flower in the Sidewalk'**?" *Mabel asked.*

"Good try, but that's a little lame, Grandma. I think I'll call it **'One Foot In Front of the Other'**," *Sonja said, studying the painting at arms length.*

"I'm confused," *Mabel said.* "There are no feet in the picture. Why would you call it one foot in front of the other?"

"It's a metaphor, Grandma." *Sonja put her hands on her hips and stood akimbo. Mabel braced herself. Whenever Sonja positioned her body like that, Mabel knew she was in for a full blown lesson on some topic near and dear to Sonja's heart.*

"You see, Grandma, a metaphor represents an idea or concept. I think the flower that has grown through the concrete represents the idea that even though our circumstances may be dreary and undesirable, we can still push our way through and be beautiful if we stay focused and just put one foot in front of the other every day." Sonja was animated as she continued with her explanation. "I think this painting tells the story of how we can handle anything and also a story of succeeding in the face of great adversity."

As she stood with her eyes closed, a tear rolled down Mabel's cheek. At a loss for words, "wow" was all she could manage to say. She was extremely proud of the way her granddaughter had grown into such a wise young woman.

Sonja looked intently at Mabel. Putting her thumbs end to end, her index fingers pointed straight up as she made a frame of Mabel's face.

"I think I'll call this one '**Something I Will Never See Again**'," she exclaimed, laughing.

"What are you talking about?" Mabel opened her eyes in surprise.

"You were actually at a loss for words, Grandma. You were speechless! I don't think I will ever see that again."

"Let's hope not," Mabel replied and they had a good laugh together.

GRANDMA MABEL'S WISDOM

Sonja's observation about the painting provided evidence of her budding insight about life. Mabel was proud that her granddaughter understood that sometimes life hands us difficult circumstances, but we can overcome and grow tall, straight, and beautiful like the flower in the painting. If we focus on putting one foot in front of the other, one day at a time and one choice at a time, we will find that each succeeding step and each succeeding choice becomes less difficult. We become stronger because of this process, and soon we can find that we have developed a set of habits that lead to success, peace, and joy in our lives.

Congratulations! You have completed the Decision Reframing Process. Many clients tell me that they actually feel lighter after being relieved from the burdens that they carried around for so long.

You are a very different person from when you first picked up this book. Unfortunately, you are also a creature of habit. As you go through your daily activities, you might find yourself falling back on some old ways of speaking about yourself and about the world. For example, if you were afraid of spiders before you let go of your stored fear, you may be accustomed to saying, "I am so afraid of spiders!" But I'll bet if you really stopped to think about how you actually feel about spiders right now, you won't be able to generate the old feelings of fear.

The final phase of this program is provided so that you can replace old habits with new ways of speaking and behaving. By completing the journal on the next few pages, you will call attention to yourself when you are falling back into old habits. You will also pay attention to the small successes that you will have every day.

For the next four weeks, be an astute observer of your life throughout the day. At the end of the day make notes about your observations. In week one, you will simply notice situations where you might have felt one of the old emotions that you released. Notice how your feelings have changed, and record the difference in your journal for that day.

In week two, continue the focus of week one but add to your observations any behavior that is new for you. If you had held yourself back in some areas of your life and now you find that you are moving forward, make a note in your journal at the end of each day as evidence of this progress. Or, perhaps you didn't do something that you would have done in the past and not acting or speaking was the better choice. Record that success also.

In week three, record at least one thing that happens in each day of that week that made you happy or brought you a feeling of joy and fulfillment. Of course, you can record more than one situation. The more you have to record, the better!

In week four, the final week of this exercise, record thoughts you have about the future and any plans you make for the future. Also, record the steps you take each day to put your plans in motion and any results that you experience from your planning.

BETTER CHOICES

Your life is built on every decision that you have made until this very moment—from the decision to get out of bed, to what you will have for breakfast, to the kind of day you expect to experience. You make the decision, and then you spend the rest of the day defending and justifying your choice.

My hope is that your experience with this book has led you to make every choice count toward a happy and fulfilling life. You have reframed the way you made choices in the past and learned a way to take responsibility for creating your own happiness at every moment. You are prepared to add your name to the list of those who can shout, "*I love my life.*" It's time to be at cause, drive your own bus, and live your life from the inside out. You now know that you can do it.

Just do it all and have a great life!

PERSONAL FOUR-WEEK GUIDED JOURNAL

How to use this Journal

You have learned many new things about yourself as you cleared the stored negative emotions and limiting decisions from your past with the Balloon Process™. You have a new perspective that will allow you to embrace each day with a sense of peace, confidence and joy. This journal is a tool to assist your integration and continued growth. Writing in your journal each day will give you a deeper connection with the new person that you have become.

Journaling is simply the process of putting into words your thoughts and feelings and writing those words on down the following pages. It is sometimes helpful to play soothing music in the background as you write.

If you enjoyed the music on the Better Choices Companion CDs, I suggest you visit our website at *www. betterchoicesbook.com* for information on downloading the instrumental MP3 file or for ordering the instrumental CD by Marlon Stokes.

As you journal, you will focus on a different theme in each of the next four weeks. In week one, I'd like you to spend the week observing the many ways in which you view the world through a different set of lenses. Pay particular attention to situations in which you may have felt anger, hurt, fear, or guilt in the past. Notice what a difference the absence of these emotions makes when you are faced with those familiar situations.

In week two, continue to observe and record the changes in your feelings as you did in week one. In addition, notice and record any new behavior or habits that you have adopted. Write your observations during a quiet moment at the end of each day.

Week three will allow you the opportunity to continue with the points of observation from weeks one and two and, additionally, to record at least one thing that happens in each day of that week that makes you happy or brings you a feeling of joy and fulfillment. Of course, you can record more than one situation. The more you have to record, the better!

By week four, you will have become comfortable with your new way of life. During this week, pay close attention to your thoughts about the future and any plans you make for the future. Also record the steps you take each day to put your plans in motion and any results that you experience from your planning.

A note of caution—journaling may bring up some issues that you have not resolved. If you notice some emotions or limiting decisions that were not released, return to the appropriate chapter and work through the DRP™ process again. Do this as many times as you feel it is necessary.

Have fun with your journaling! Enjoy this process and congratulate yourself on the positive changes you have made and those that you will continue to make in the future. And if you would like to share your stories of success with me, I would love to hear them. You can email me at *fayehargrove@betterchoicesbook.com.*

Week One: Notice situations where you might have felt one of the old emotions that you released. Pay attention to how your feelings have changed and record the difference in your journal for that day. This week, simply observe your feelings and record your observations.

Day 1 _____

_____

_____

_____

_____

Day 2 _____

_____

_____

_____

_____

Day 3 _____

_____

_____

_____

_____

Day 4 _____

_____

_____

_____

_____

Day 5 _____

_____

_____

_____

_____

Day 6 _____

_____

_____

_____

_____

Day 7 _____

_____

_____

_____

_____

_____

_____

Week Two: Continue the focus of week one (observe and record) and add to your observations any behavior that is new for you. For example, if you had held yourself back in some areas of your life and now you find that you are moving forward, make a note in your journal at the end of each day as evidence of this progress. Or, perhaps you didn't do something that you would have done in the past and not acting or speaking was the better choice. Record that success also.

Day 1 _____

_____

_____

_____

_____

_____

Day 2 _____

_____

_____

_____

_____

_____

Day 3 _____

_____

_____

_____

_____

_____

Day 4 _____

_____

_____

_____

_____

Day 5 _____

_____

_____

_____

_____

Day 6 _____

_____

_____

_____

_____

Day 7 _____

_____

_____

_____

_____

Week Three: *Record at least one thing that happens in each day of this week that made you happy or brought you a feeling of joy and fulfillment. Of course, you can record more than one situation. The more you have to record, the better!*

Day 1 _____

_____

_____

_____

_____

Day 2 _____

_____

_____

_____

_____

Day 3 _____

_____

_____

_____

_____

_____

Day 4 _____

_____

_____

_____

_____

Day 5 _____

_____

_____

_____

_____

Day 6 _____

_____

_____

_____

_____

Day 7 _____

_____

_____

_____

_____

_____

Week Four: Record thoughts you have about the future and any plans you make for the future. Also, record the steps you take each day to put your plans in motion and any results that you experience from your planning.

Day 1 _____

_____

_____

_____

_____

Day 2 _____

_____

_____

_____

_____

Day 3 _____

_____

_____

_____

_____

_____

Day 4 _____

_____

_____

_____

_____

_____

Day 5 _____

_____

_____

_____

_____

_____

Day 6 _____

_____

_____

_____

_____

_____

Day 7 _____

_____

_____

_____

_____

_____

Appendix
BETTER CHOICES Companion CDs
Track Listings

Track Contents Companion CD 1

Track 1 (0:23)	*Welcome*
Track 2 (4:19)	*Better Choices is the Goal*
Track 3 (3:48)	*How to work with the CD's*
Track 4 (1:57)	*Your Unconscious Mind and Memories*
Track 5 (1:45)	*Noticing How You Store Time*
Track 6 (1:05)	*Make Notes about Your Timeline*
Track 7 (3:59)	*Test Drive on Your Timeline*
Track 8 (2:58)	*Describing the Process- the Timeline*
Track 9 (2:25)	*Describing the Process- Floating*
Track 10 (2:57)	*Describing the Process – Get the Lesson*
Track 11 (1:51)	*Points to Remember About Anger*
Track 12 (0:46)	*Write "I feel Angry About..."*
Track 13 (1:08)	*What Would Happen If I Did?*
Track 14 (1:35)	*Root Cause for Anger*
Track 15 (7:07)	*Clearing Out the Anger*
Track 16 (1:11)	*Note the Learnings about Anger*
Track 17 (0:55)	*No Anger-Now What?*
Track 18 (1:34)	*Causes of Sadness*
Track 19 (1:48)	*A Note About Grief*
Track 20 (1:58)	*Write "I Feel Sad About..."*
Track 21 (1:31)	*Root Cause for Sadness*
Track 22 (5:59)	*Clearing Out the Sadness*
Track 23 (1:09)	*Notice Your Feelings Have Changed*
Track 24 (2:19)	*What is Fear?*
Track 25 (1:43)	*Write "I Feel Fearful About..."*
Track 26 (1:39)	*Root Cause for Fear*
Track 27 (5:58)	*Clearing out the Fear*
Track 28 (1:24)	*Record the Learnings About Fear*

Track Contents Companion CD 2